ARCHITECTS IN AMERICA
of
CATHOLIC TRADITION

ARCHITECTS IN AMERICA

of

CATHOLIC TRADITION

By

FRANCIS W. KERVICK

ARCHITECT
F. R. S. A.

CHARLES E. TUTTLE COMPANY: PUBLISHERS
Rutland, Vermont

European Representative
BOXERBOOKS, INC., Zurich

Published by the
Charles E. Tuttle Company
of Rutland, Vermont & Tokyo, Japan
with editorial offices at
15 Edogawa-cho, Bunkyo-ku, Tokyo

Library of Congress
Catalog Card No. 61–14032

First edition, 1962

MANUFACTURED IN JAPAN

*To those men who tried to
create beauty by
following
The Architect of The Universe.*

*Wisdom 44: 1–15
—and there are some of whom there is no
memorial; who are perished as if they had never been
born, and their children with them.
May light eternal shine upon them, O Lord,
with Thy saints forever.*

TABLE OF CONTENTS

LIST OF ILLUSTRATIONS

8

INTRODUCTION

IN PREPARING a biography of Patrick Charles Keely on the occasion of the centennial of his coming to this country in 1842 it was surprising to find that there was a great lack of material concerning a man who for fifty years had been thought of whenever any ecclesiastical work was to be done. If such a man could be forgotten in a half century it seemed worthwhile to record, as far as possible, other men who might be thus forgotten.

There was also the interesting question of whether these men had followed the precedent of their Catholic ancestors. When one considers that all the important buildings from the fall of Rome to the religious revolt of the 16th century had been the work of Catholic architects it was of interest to compare the later men with these masters.

The period of American architecture is not long as it is only from the Revolution to the present day and it is only in these one hundred and eighty years that records of Catholic architects or of any architects can be found.

While it is true that Catholics had made the first explorations in what is now the United States, the settlements along the Atlantic coast were not permanent. Verrazano had explored the waters about what is now New York City; he had landed on the feast of Saints Peter and Paul on the island which he gave the name of the Apostles Island and which is now known as Long Island and other Spaniards had penetrated as far north as Virginia but such settlements were not maintained.

When in the early decades of the 17th century the English landed and made settlements in Virginia and New England, they unfortunately brought with them the penal laws of the Elizabethan period. Catholics were not wanted and if found were to be treated with the same severity as in the homeland.

The French had come into northern New England and there was constant warfare between them and the English settlers. The French had as well explored the vast territory of the Mississippi Valley and the lands about the Great Lakes. On the Gulf of Mexico both French and Spanish settlers were to be found and in the southwest the country was familiar ground to the Spanish from the days of Father Kino.

Here the religious communities of priests or friars and their converted Indians numbering many thousands had established missions. For these converts buildings had been constructed of stone or in many cases of sun-dried bricks. Few of these can be considered as the work of architects trained in the profession but each was erected under the supervision and general layout of the superior of the mission. The quality of design varied according to the knowledge of the superior and the skill of the Indians who had been trained in all branches of building and the arts of painting and ornament. Thus it has been considered well to record in this book the names of priests who were outstanding in their building.

Such were the conditions existing in the country until the fourth decade of the 19th century. Then great numbers of Irish emigrants began to appear due to the impoverished conditions in their own country. The effects of the penal laws were still to be seen for men and women had been denied all forms of education; the professions were closed to them and in the new world only the roughest work was available. The Germans who left their homes due to the revolutions and the persecutions of the 1840's were in better condition. They came educated, many in the professions, and occupied places of standing.

However, priests were few and large churches were thus a necessity so that as many as possible might be present at one time for Mass. Often a former non-Catholic church might be available to buy and to be remodelled for use but there were few Catholic architects available in the states at the time.

In 1842, Patrick Keely came to this country and settled in Brooklyn. He had worked as a carpenter for his father who was a builder in Kilkenny, Ireland. For several years Keely followed his trade in Brooklyn until an opportunity was given to him to design a church in the Williamsburgh section of Brooklyn. In this he pleased both the pastor and the congregation so that commissions came to him from all parts east of the Mississippi and from New Orleans to Montreal. For fifty years he had almost the entire work of the Irish parishes.

About New York, Cincinnati and Milwaukee Germans were numerous and architects of the same nationality were designing their churches and religious structures. These buildings were largely based upon a Romanesque tradition while the Irish parish churches were more often influenced by the work of Pugin. Much of the work shows the scanty resources of the people. Gothic forms were used but the general effect was gained by the aid of lath and plaster. There were few craftsmen either in wood or stone and any glass had to be obtained in Europe where in that period of the 19th century such art was at a very low level.

The teaching of architecture in schools was only beginning. There were courses offered in architectural subjects at Columbia, Notre Dame and Harvard, but the students of the 1860's had to go to Paris. From this time on American architecture began to show an improvement. The Romanesque of Richardson had little effect upon Catholic builders possibly due to the fact that it was an expensive form even in those days.

From the end of the 19th century well into the 20th century improvements are to be noted. Catholics were receiving the training available to those of means; the position of the Church was also improving and there were many opportunities to build churches and colleges. Then too, the craftsmen were developing and there were a number of good glass designers who were able to add the beauty of fine glass to many churches.

In this development the influence of Ralph Adams Cram should not be overlooked. Although not a Catholic, he pointed out in a dozen books the great work of the Catholic builders of medieval times. Probably no other American architect did so much to raise the level of design in both non-Catholic and Catholic work. For the non-Catholic he brought the designers to the realization of the beauty and convenience of the church plan of their Catholic ancestors and for the Catholic architects it was his influence that brought to this country many competent craftsmen in wood, metal and stone.

The record of architects of Catholic background that follows records in some measure what these architects of the past century and a half have contributed to the culture of the United States.

Acknowledgment of help in supplying information is gratefully made to the libraries, chancery offices, and public officials without whose assistance this volume would not have been possible.

The help of the following in giving permission for the use of photographs is also acknowledged: National Gallery; Rockefeller Centre; Connecticut College for Women; Historical Societies of Philadelphia, Missouri; Union College; *The Detroit News*; The New Orleans Historical Library.

ARCHITECTS IN AMERICA
of
CATHOLIC TRADITION

THE ARCHITECTS

ROLLAND ADELSPERGER was born October 9, 1871 at La Porte, Indiana. He studied at Armour Institute of Technology in Chicago and the Art Institute. He received the A. B. degree at Notre Dame in 1890 and later the degree of B. S. He was an officer in the army during the Spanish war and later was in charge of hospitals and charitable buildings in Cuba. From 1905 until 1914 he was Dean of the College of Architecture at Notre Dame. He also maintained an office in South Bend, Ind. Later he was a professor of architecture at the Texas Agricultural and Mechanical College and was a member of the Chicago Architectural Club. Died in 1930.

RAYMOND ALMIRALL was born in Brooklyn, N.Y. in 1869. He was graduated from the Brooklyn Polytechnic Institute and later attended Cornell University. He then went to the Ecole des Beaux Arts in Paris where he received his diploma in 1896. He had an extensive practice in New York and during that time he acted as architectural consultant for the libraries of Brooklyn.

From 1904 until 1914 he designed all the branch libraries of Brooklyn and made a design for the Central library but this design was not followed. In 1908 he was appointed by Governor Theodore Roosevelt to be a member of the Tenement Commission of New York City.

During this period he designed many religious and institutional buildings such as the Novitiate of The Little Sisters of the Poor in Brooklyn; the hospitals in the Bronx, Fordham, Jamaica and Sea View on Long Island; the church of The Nativity and Saint Michael's church, school and rectory in Brooklyn. In World War I he was in service in France. In 1924 he returned there where he was active in the restoration of historic buildings. For his work on the palaces of Versailles and Trianon he was created a Chevalier of the Legion of Honor. Died October 18, 1939.

DON ANDRE ALMANASTER Y ROXAS while not in practice as an architect is reputed to have been the architect and builder of the Cabildo in New Orleans. It is probable that he had for this work the aid of the adjutant of the Plaza, Gilbert Guilleman. For the Cathedral of Saint Louis in New Orleans which faces the former Plaza, now Jackson Square, he gave the funds and built the church. Here for many years it was the custom to commemorate his gift by the celebration of Mass each Saturday.

His daughter, the Countess Pontalba, did much to beautify this part of the city by building the Pontalba Apartments and improving the Plaza which through her influence was named Jackson Square in honor of the hero of the battle of New Orleans. Don Almanaster died April 26, 1798 at the age of seventy-four.

PETER AMARI was born in Brooklyn, N. Y., May 22, 1913. He studied at Pratt Institute in Brooklyn and at New York University where he received the degree in architecture. During his active years he was

13

employed by such firms as Waid and Corbett; Voorhees, Walker, Foley and Smith and by Polhemus and Coffin, all of New York City.

A member of the New York Chapter of the A.I.A. Died January 10, 1953.

HARRY M. AMBROSE was born in 1902 in Logan, Ohio. In 1925 he received the degree in architecture at the University of Notre Dame and in 1927 began working in the Office of Public Buildings in Washington, D.C. He was employed upon the projects of building the National Institute of Health and the Washington Hospital Center.

Before his death he was working upon the Central Intelligence Agency building at Langley, Va. For this work he received a meritorious service award from the General Services Administration.

He was a member of the Notre Dame Club of Washington and the Manor Country Club. Died in Washington Feb. 9, 1959.

WILFRID EDWARDS ANTHONY was born Nov. 16, 1877 at Orient, N. Y., the son of Frederick H. and Anna W. Edwards. He was a descendent of the noted American clergyman, Jonathan Edwards. He was educated in the public and private schools of Brooklyn and then worked in architectural offices in New York. In 1900 he became a Catholic and entered the employ of Cram and Ferguson, where he remained until 1920.

In his work he had much to do with the design of ecclesiastical buildings and he was considered a gifted designer of interior fittings and decoration of churches.

He was a member of Saint Hilda's Guild where he did similar work for it and contributed to many journals.

In his own practice he was the architect of many important schools and churches. Among these are Saint Catherine of Siena on West 66th Street; Corpus Christi church on 121st Street, both in New York City. In the latter church he showed the appropriate use of Georgian architecture for Catholic churches as he did also in Holy Cross College chapel in Washington, D. C. He worked in River Forest, Ill. for the Dominican Fathers and at Dun Scotus College in Detroit, Michigan for the Franciscan Fathers. Died July 25, 1948.

EPHRAIM FRANCIS BALDWIN was born in Troy, N. Y. October 4, 1837, the son of an engineer who later moved his family to Baltimore. He was educated in the public schools and at Mount Saint Mary's College in Emmitsburg, Md. He studied architecture and engineering at Rensselaer Polytechnic Institute in Troy and then returned to Baltimore where he worked for John Niernsee and later with Bruce Price. With the latter he worked on the designs for Christ Episcopal Church and then became associated with Josiah Pennington.

The firm did much ecclesiastical work. In Baltimore they did the churches of Saint Gregory; Saint Mary, Star of The Sea; Our Lady of Good Counsel; Saint Ann; Saint Patrick; Saint Wencelas; Saint Mary's Orphan Asylum and the Convent of the Little Sisters of the Poor. In Emmitsburgh they did the college church and the seminary. In Wilmington the church of Saint Ann. In Washington the firm did the churches of Saint Mary and Saint Augustine; the Divinity Hall at Catholic University and in Germantown, Pa. the church of The Immaculate Conception.

At Annapolis the Circular Court of Appeals; the restoration of the old State House and the annex.

PLATE I. Dun Scotus College, Detroit, Michigan. Wilfred E. Anthony, Architect. (Photograph by The Detroit News.)

In Baltimore the Hotel Rennert; McCoy Hall at Johns Hopkins University; the City Hospital and Polyclinic Hospital and the Sun Office Building. Died March 21, 1916.

LOUIS J. BARBOT was brought from Santo Domingo to Charleston, S. C. where he was reared and educated. He attended the German Friendly Society School and then entered the Charleston High School where he showed marked attainment in languages, science and mathematics. After his graduation he continued studies in classics and French with Father Carr and the Abbe Fillon. It was intended that he would go to France to study with the astronomer Arago but circumstances prevented this. He then began to study with E. C. Jones, one of the important architects of that period in Charleston. He worked also with Werner and with John H. Seyle, an outstanding architect.

In 1850 he was employed on railroad and canal surveys rising from working as a rodman to the assistant engineer in charge. This gave him work upon a number of railroads such as the Columbia and Augusta Railroad and the Edisto and Ashley River Canal. He was asked to become the City Civil Engineer and was elected in March 1837, which position he held for thirty-six years.

During the Civil War he had a brilliant record in the Confederate army and rose to the rank of captain of artillery. He was stationed at Fort Moultrie. Later as military engineer he did much in strengthening the fortifications at many places until the end of the war.

After his parole in 1865 he returned to Charleston to resume his practice. He was a member of the board of the council of engineering societies and President of the Southern Society of Civil Engineers.

DECIMUS CHARTRAND BARBOT, the son of Charles Decimus and Maria Luisa Chartrand Barbot was born Dec. 11, 1873 on a plantation on the Elizabeth River which is now a part of the city of Norfolk, Va. He was brought as a child to Charleston and studied with his uncle Louis Barbot. After the removal of Louis Barbot to Augusta, Ga. the nephew was for a number of years Assistant City Engineer and in 1910 opened his office for architectural practice.

Bishop Northrop employed him to design the interior of the Cathedral of Charleston. Later he was architect for Saint Anthony's Church in Florence, S. C.; the Catholic church in Sumter, S. C.; the Knights of Columbus Hall; the Victory Theatre and the Bishop England High School in Charleston; many private houses; the remodelling of the Charleston High School and the County Court House.

His later years were spent in Hyattsville, Md. where he died Dec. 31, 1934, his grave being in Saint Lawrence Cemetery in Charleston.

CHARLES BARTHBERGER was born in Baden, Germany in 1823 where he was graduated from the Polytechnic Institute in Carlsruhe in 1843. He came to the United States in 1845 and settled in Pittsburgh. Here he became favorably known throughout the western part of Pennsylvania and eastern Ohio. He worked on the Cathedral of Pittsburgh and the church of Saint Philomena which was completed in 1865. He was a member of the A.I.A. and died August 8, 1896.

His son of the same name was associated with his father.

GEORGE DENNIS BARNETT was born in Saint Louis in 1863 the son of George I. Barnett who had come from England where he received his training in architecture. The son was educated by the Christian Brothers and then entered his father's office. From there he became the chief draftsman for the Saint

PLATE II. Mount Royal Station, Baltimore, Maryland. Baldwin & Pennington, Architects. (Photograph by Detroit Photographic Co. Reproduced from the Collections of the Library of Congress.)

Louis Building Department. In 1889 he began to practice architecture in association with his brother-in-law, John Haynes and later with his brother Tom.

From 1907 until 1914 they worked upon the new Cathedral of Saint Louis and in addition upon such buildings as the Visitation Convent at Cabanne Street and Belt Avenue and the Hotel Lafayette at Little Rock, Ark. In 1911 Tom Barnett established his own office and George Barnett went to Los Angeles where he practiced for a period before his death in 1925.

TOM BARNETT also born in Saint Louis, March 11, 1870, the youngest son of G. I. Barnett. He was educated at Washington University and then entered his father's office. After that he was with his brother and brother-in-law until he established his own office. Alone he was the architect of the Arcade Building in Saint Louis, the Busch Memorial; New City Club; Eden Theological Seminary at Webster Grove and the Kirby Building in Dallas, Texas.

Later he retired to devote his time to painting and became well known. From 1914 until 1925 he received five times the first prize of the Ives Medal from the Saint Louis Artists' Guild. At the Portland Exposition in 1905 he received a bronze medal for painting and at the Saint Louis Exposition in 1904 a gold medal. A member of the A.I.A. Died September 23, 1929.

JOHN BEHAN, an early architect in Pittsburgh, is reputed to have designed the first Cathedral begun in 1828.

LOUIS BEEZER was born in 1869 and practiced in Pittsburgh for several years with his brother and they were the architects for the church of Saint John the Baptist. They later moved to San Francisco and Louis Beezer was the architect for the Dominican church of Saint Dominic and for many buildings on the Pacific coast. He died in 1924.

FRANCIS J. BERLENBACH was for many years settled in Brooklyn, N. Y. In 1880 he was in the office of Renwick and then began an independent practice. Some of his buildings were the churches of Saint Finbar; The Assumption; Saint Joseph and The Blessed Sacrament. He was the architect for the Dominican Sisters and acted as consultant to the church authorities in architectural matters. Died in 1944.

CLAUDE BEROUJON, who was born in France, came to Mobile as a seminarian with a kinsman, Bishop Portier, the first bishop of the See. He showed so much ability at design and building that he was working for a number of years upon the buildings that were needed for the new diocese. He acted as the architect, the builder and even supervised the making of brick and the cutting of the trees to provide the wood for these structures.

One of the first buildings that he was called upon to design was for the college now known as Spring Hill. He designed a building suited for the climate and in a Roman character. Unfortunately during the absence of the Bishop changes were made greatly to the distress of Beroujon and not until many years later was this mistake corrected.

He designed the Convent for the Visitation nuns in 1832, the Cathedral rectory, and made designs for the Cathedral. His health failed and as a result he relinquished his desire for the priesthood. He continued his work in architecture confining himself to church work. The Cathedral which was completed in

PLATE III. St. Louis Cathedral, St. Louis, Missouri. Barnett, Haynes and Barnett, Architects. (Photograph by Woodward & Tiernan. Reproduced from the Collections of the Library of Congress.)

1849 was designed in a Roman Corinthian style and was of considerable size being 165 feet in length and with a frontage of 102 feet. When Spring Hill College was rebuilt he was joined by James Freret of New Orleans whose family has always been staunch supporters of this school.

Beroujon married a member of the O'Neill family of Mobile and his descendents were long settled in the city.

JOHN H. BESARICK of Boston was the architect of the Theology and Philosophy Houses built in the 1880's for Saint John's Seminary in Brighton and also the first house for the Archbishop.

WILLIAM BESARICK at this period was also practicing in Boston.

CHARLES BICKEL was born in Columbus, Ohio in 1852 where he was educated and then continued study in Europe. In 1875 he worked in Philadelphia before going to Pittsburgh where with John F. Brennan he opened an office. Their practice was largely in commercial work. A member of the A.I.A. Died Feb. 1, 1921.

CASIMIR J. BIEGALSKI was born in Chicago in 1906 and was graduated from Armour Institute of Technology. He studied design at Catholic University and engineering defense at George Washington University.

For twenty four years he was in the General Services Administration and was the consulting member with the architects of the projects of the National Institute of Health. He was assistant chief of the hospital unit, design and construction division and acted as the specialist in design in hospital work. He worked on the National Health Service hospitals throughout the country, the Washington Hospital Center and Saint Elizabeth Hospital. A member of the A.I.A. and registered in Virginia, Maryland and the District of Columbia. Died Oct. 23, 1957.

ALBERT M. BIELAWSKI was born in Poland in 1867 and at twenty-five became an American citizen. He was prominent in politics. In Cudahy, Wis. he was City Clerk before coming to Michigan where he settled in 1915. In 1928 he was the only Democrat elected to the legislature and the first of his party to sit in the legislature for sixteen years. Died June 20, 1942.

EVERETT A. BLACKMAN was born in Paris, Ill. and after his early education he was graduated in architecture from Notre Dame in 1917. He served as a lieutenant in the First World War and then worked in Indianapolis before opening an office in Danville, Ill. where he spent the rest of his life. He was the architect for many schools, industrial buildings and public buildings that included the City Hall of Danville. During his career of thirty years he received many evidences of the high regard of the citizens of the city. Died September 4, 1954.

JAMES F. BLY was born in 1887 and studied at Pratt Institute where he received an architectural degree and later an engineering degree at Columbia University.

He worked in offices in Brooklyn and Queens and became an inspector for the Federal Housing Authority and in 1942 chief underwriter of the New York office.

PLATE IV. Archbishopric, New Orleans, Louisiana. Graton Chamellon, Architect. (Reproduced from the Collections of the Library of Congress.)

His firm, Bly and Namann, did much work such as housing. He had been one of the ten architects who drew plans for the Ten Eyck Houses in the Williamsburg section of Brooklyn and was also a consultant for a builder.

In earlier years he served in the State Assembly and was a member of the Kings County Republican County Committee. A former President of the New York Society of Architects; the Brooklyn Architects Club; the Long Island Society of Architects. Died July 29, 1959.

ROMOLO BOTTELLI was born in 1875 and was educated in Newark, N. J. where he was employed for a number of years before opening his own office in 1898. He did a large amount of residential, commercial and industrial designing especially apartment houses. He died June 4, 1957.

EDWARD BOYLE of New York was an architect and engineer and among his buildings is the chapel at Calvary Cemetery, New York.

EDWARD BOYLE was born in Shelton, Conn. September 15, 1904. After his graduation from Shelton High School he was a student at Pratt Institute in Brooklyn and later in the School of Architecture at Yale. For many years he was Chief Architect for the Federal Housing Authority in Hartford. Died March 16, 1957.

THOMAS BRADY was born in Ireland in 1829 and established an office in Saint Louis in 1865. In 1870 he joined John Mitchell who was considered to be one of the city's outstanding architects. He was architect for the church at the University of Notre Dame and in Saint Louis the synagogue known as the Temple of the Gates of Truth.

CHARLES A. BREHMER was born in Glencoe, Ill. Sept. 21, 1860. Educated in the local schools until he came to the University of Notre Dame. Later he worked for his father who was in the lumber business and then went to Evansville, Ind. where he became a partner of Clifford Shopbell and early architect there. In 1897 he opened an office in South Bend and devoted himself to the design of schools and churches. Member of the Young Mens' Institute and the Knights of Saint John. Died 1909.

THOMAS F. BRENNAN was born in Philadelphia in 1857 and was educated there at La Salle College. Later he went to Pittsburgh where he was trained in architecture. He joined Charles Bickel and among the buildings designed by the firm were the Home of the Little Sisters of the Poor and the German National Bank. A member of the A.I.A. Died June 11, 1925.

ERHARD BRIELMAIER was born in Wuertenberg, Germany and when about six was brought to America where his father was a builder in Cincinnati. He came to Milwaukee and there began a practice which with his sons has lasted nearly a century. One of his important buildings is the Basilica of Saint Josephat which is one of the notable buildings in the city.

JOSEPH BRIELMAIER, one of the sons of Erhard who followed in his father's practice, was born in 1880 and at an early age entered his father's office where he spent the rest of his life in the large practice

22

PLATE V. St. Luke's Church, St. Paul, Minnesota. John T. Comes, Architect.

that had developed over the years. He was registered in eight states and one of his notable buildings is Saint Benedict's Abbey in Atchinson, Kansas. Died Dec. 13, 1953.

WILLIAM BRINKMAN worked in Chicago in the first decade of the twentieth century and during a brief life was architect of such buildings as Walsh Hall at the University of Notre Dame and Holy Cross Church in Chicago. He died in 1910.

PETER BRUST was born in the vicinity of Milwaukee in 1869 and was educated in the local parish schools. His architectural training was received in Milwaukee offices and he felt a particular regard for the careful training he received from George Ferry who was one of the prominent architects of the city. Later with a group of students he travelled in Europe making sketches and photographs.

In 1906 he opened an office with Richard Phillip which was maintained for twenty years until he was joined by his sons, Paul and John, who still maintain the office.

With Mr. Phillip he designed Kohler Village and the church of Saint John in that village, the Sacred Heart Sanitarium in Milwaukee, the Alvernia High School in Chicago, the office buildings for the Wisconsin Telephone Company and buildings for Saint Francis Seminary in Milwaukee.

During his career he received a number of professional appointments such as Regional Director of the Illinois-Wisconsin district of the A.I.A. from 1940 to 1943; Director of the Wisconsin chapter of the A.I.A. and President of the chapter for several terms; a member of the Mayor's Advisory Council for five years; a member for ten years of the Art Commission and for eighteen years a member of the Board of Appeals on Zoning. A Fellow of the A.I.A. Died June 20, 1946.

MARC ISAMBARD BRUNEL was born April 25, 1769 at Hoqueville near Gisors in Normandy. His family had been farmers for many generations but his education was under the supervision of his uncle, a priest. When eight he was sent to the College of Gisors with the expectation that he was to enter the priesthood. Later he was sent to the Seminary of Saint Nicais at Rouen. He had so marked a taste for drawing and mechanical studies and so little inclination for theological courses that he left the Seminary and entered the navy where he served for six years. Because of the French Revolution he came to New York September 6, 1793 and worked as a civil engineer. During this time he surveyed the line of the canal between Lake Champlain and the Hudson River. He became an American citizen and lived for a period in New York City. He was associated with the Mangin brothers on the design of the Park Theatre in 1798 and worked with his countryman, Major Charles L'Enfant, upon other buildings.

Later he left the country and settled in London where he became known for outstanding engineering projects, both civil and mechanical. He was engineer for the Thames Tunnel and was knighted for his many achievements. His death occurred in 1844. His son Marc Kingdom Brunel was architect for the Paddington Station built one hundred years ago and who has been called the greatest engineer of the 19th century.

JOSEPH Z. BURGEE was born in Saint Louis in 1897 and attended the University of Illinois. During the invasion of Mexico in 1916 he served in the army and also served in the First World War. He came to Chicago and became a member of the office of Holabird and Root and in 1945 he became a partner.

During the Second World War he was special advisor in the office of production management in

PLATE VI. Beauregard House, 1113 Chartres Street, New Orleans, Louisiana. Francois Correjolles, Architect. (Reproduced from the Collections of the Library of Congress.

25

1941 and 1942. While associated with Holabird and Root he was identified with many notable buildings such as the American Bar Association headquarters; buildings at the University of Notre Dame; Northwestern University; County Building at Madison, Wis.; the Canadian National Terminal in Montreal; the Teamsters' Union Building in Washington; the Tata Research Building in Bombay; hotels in Venezuela and Columbia. He was advisor to the Chicago Lake Front Fair and was working on the Chicago Exposition Center.

He served on boards of the Cancer Research Hospital; the Notre Dame Foundation; Chicago Catholic Charities and was Chairman of the Committee of Civil Defense. On a business trip to New York he died suddenly in 1955.

JOHN J. BURNS was born in New York City in 1881. He was graduated from Washington University and spent most of his professional life in Chicago. He was engaged with his partners in designing theatres and some churches. The new Saint Peter's church in Chicago was the product of his office. Died Dec. 14, 1956.

BERNARD J. S. CAHILL was born in London in 1866 the son of James Alban and Eliza Smith Cahill. He was educated at Ratcliffe College of the University of London in 1884 and at Kensington School of Art in 1887. At twenty he came to this country and opened an office in San Francisco and Oakland. He was the architect for buildings on the Pacific coast as far north as Vancouver. Among the buildings were the catacombs and columbarium in Cypress Lawn Cemetery and that of Saint Mary in Sacramento; the Multonomah Hotel in Portland, Ore.; the Drummond Head Memorial Park in Honolulu. He was interested in town planning and attended the London Town Planning conferences in 1909 and the conference on town planning in 1910. His plan for the Civic Center in San Francisco made in 1904 was adopted in 1912. From 1899 to 1935 he invented the butterfly map: an octahedral system of projection used in meteorology geophysics which was adopted by the Pan American Airway. He wrote upon architectural subjects and cartography and in 1906 was editor of the American Builder Review. Died Oct. 4, 1944.

FATHER ANTONIO CALZADO was born in Florida, Nov. 24, 1760 and came to California in October 1787 where he died at Santa Inez, Dec. 23, 1814.

FATHER JOHN M. CAMBIASO, S. J. was born of a noble Genoese family who was living in Lyons, France. He received much of his early education at the Jesuit College in Lyons and at nineteen entered the Society of Jesus. For a number of years he taught in France, Sardinia, Africa and Spain and it was probably due to this environment that he became an admirer of Moresque work.

He was sent as a Visitor to represent Father Jordan, the Superior of the Province of Lyons in New Orleans, and he remained as the head of the mission. He showed great industry in literary and philosophical studies as well as an interest in astronomy and building. When the church he started in Baronne Street was completed he built in back of the dome an observatory. Later he was appointed a Visitor to Mexico and upon returning to the United States in 1851 he began a new church which he designed and for which his relatives in Europe supplied the funds.

His interest in building and engineering stood him in good stead for the church was built on what had

PLATE VII. Duncker Hall, Washington University, St. Louis, Missouri. Angelo Corrubia, Architect.

been a cypress swamp. An effort to lighten the load was made by building piers with iron columns so that the intervening walls had only their own weight to support. Between the pilasters and walls, front towers and facade slip joints were used. In spite of these precautions, settlement took place so that the upper part of the buildings was of wood with iron bars. The roof and sides were of copper sheets laid upon rods. The interior shows his interest in Arabic design as the pews have iron ends with figures of The Blessed Virgin. The altar was designed by James Freret and at the Paris Exposition in 1867 received a first prize. The statue of The Blessed Virgin was designed by Denis Foyaties who was the sculptor of the statue of Saint Joan of Arc that stands in the Place of the Martyr in Orleans. The statue in New Orleans had been commissioned by Queen Marie Amalie, the wife of King Louis Phillipe, and was intended for her private chapel, but the overthrow of the monarchy brought the statue to America. The Stations of The Cross were painted by the Jesuit Fathers Martin and Cahier who were the authors of the monograph on the Cathedral of Bourges.

Later Father Cambiaso was President of the College of the Immaculate Conception. Died October 24, 1869.

ROSARIO CANDELA was born March 7, 1890 in Sicily. He began his architectural training there before coming to this country in 1909 and completed his studies at Columbia in 1915.

With his associate, Paul Resnick, he designed a number of Sutton Place houses; the large housing projects of Fort Greene Houses; Gowanus Houses and Forest Houses; the East Harlem and Morrisiana Health Centres and public schools.

Due to reading Poe's *The Gold Bug* he became interested in cryptology and during World War II he served with the American Intelligence unit as an expert on secret codes and ciphers. Two books on the subject were written by him. He was Honorary President of the New York Cypher Society; a member of The Architectural League of New York; the A.I.A. and the Beaux Arts Institute of Design. Died October 7, 1953.

HARRY CARR was graduated in architecture at the University of Notre Dame in 1908 and practiced for a period in Green Bay, Wis. and later removed to Evanston, Ill. where he died.

JOHN CARROLL a member of the A.I.A. died at Myrtle Beach, S. C. where he was living in retirement in 1955.

GEORGE SHEPHERDSON CHAPPELL was born in 1877 in New London, Conn. and was educated at Yale University where he received the degree of Bachelor of Architecture in 1899. Later he studied at the Ecole des Beaux Arts in Paris.

As a member of the firm of Ewing and Chappell he designed residences and the firm was the designer of the first buildings of the Connecticut College for Women at New London.

Later he abandoned architecture for literary work and journalism. Under the name of Doctor Traprock he wrote for magazines some burlesques upon the travel and exploration books of that period and upon the foibles of the times. Died Nov. 26, 1941.

JAMES E. CASALE was born in Villarosa, Italy in 1890 and at the age of ten came to the United

PLATE VIII. Pan American Union, Washington, D. C. Kelsey and Cret, Architects. (Photograph courtesy of the Pan American Union.)

States. He attended Cooper Union and Columbia. He did much work in remodelling the great houses built in New York at an earlier period and which he adapted to present day needs. He estimated that he had worked on about three thousand houses during his career. Among them were the Villiard House in Madison Avenue designed originally by McKim, Meade and White in the manner of a Florentine palace and which is now the office of Random House Publishers and the offices of the Archdiocese of New York; the Pulitzer House; the Lamont House which is now the headquarters of the Visiting Nurse Service; the Royal Dutch Airlines Building on Fifth Avenue which won the Fifth Avenue Association Award; the building for the Institute of International Education.

He belonged to the Salamagundi Club whose building he transformed; the Fifth Avenue Association; Columbia University Club; the A.I.A. and the New York Building Congress. Died July 1, 1958.

ANDRE CASTAIGNE was an architect employed in the middle of the 19th century upon the Cathedral of New Orleans.

GRATON CHAMBELLON of New Orleans was one of the architects for the Palace of the Archbishop.

MERIWETHER LEWIS CLARK was born in Saint Louis, Missouri Jan. 9, 1809. He was the son of General William Clark who with Col. Lewis had explored the North West Territory and a nephew of George Rogers Clark who had saved the upper Mississippi valley from English domination. Although he retained the spelling of Lewis his name appeared on the baptismal records of the Cathedral of Saint Louis as Louis.

He entered West Point July 1, 1825 and was graduated five years later when he was promoted to the Army as Brevet Second Lieutenant. He served at Jefferson Barracks, Mo. and later was in the Black Hawk War as Colonel. He resigned in 1833 and returned to Saint Louis where he was an architect and engineer and a member of the House of Representatives of Missouri. From 1846 to 1848 he served in the War with Mexico in command of the Battalion of Missouri Volunteers as a Major.

He was Surveyor General for the State of Missouri from 1848 to 1853. In Saint Louis he was architect for such buildings as the Church of Saint Vincent de Paul built in 1840 and which is still standing; the Shakespeare Theatre in 1837 and the Soulard House.

At the outbreak of the War in 1861 he offered his services to the Confederacy and served to the end of the war. Afterward he was Commandant of Cadets and Professor of Higher Mathematics at the Kentucky Military Institute and he was architect for Kentucky state buildings. Died Oct. 28, 1881.

NICHOLAS J. CLAYTON worked in Galveston during the last half of the 19th century. He designed the first unit of the Ursuline Convent, then the east unit in 1861 and in 1892 the central building. He was architect of the Church of The Annunciation and in New Orleans for the first Church of the Holy Redeemer; in Macon, Ga. the Church of Saint Joseph. A Fellow of the A.I.A. Died in 1918.

JOSEPH-PIERRE PICOT DE LIMOELAN DE CLORIVIERE was born November 4, 1768 of a noble family near Broons in Brittany. He was the nephew and godson of the Jesuit, Father de Cloriviere. He was educated at Rennes where he shared a room with Marceau and Chateaubriand. In 1783 at the age of fifteen he entered the army and became an officer in the guards.

PLATE IX. Church of Saint Francis de Sales, Philadelphia, Pennsylvania. H. D. Dagit, Architect.

He was a leader of the Royalists and opposed the First Consul so that he was forced to leave the country. Later with some members of his family he came in 1803 to Savannah. He was a painter of miniatures and a considerable number of these are in existence, some signed with the name of Picot and others with the name of Cloriviere. In 1808 he reached the decision to study for the priesthood and entered the Seminary in Baltimore where he was ordained in 1812. He was appointed pastor of Saint Mary's Church in Charleston, S. C. and was there except for an interval when he went to London and France in 1815. In 1819 he returned to Baltimore and was appointed that year as Director of the Convent of The Visitation in Georgetown. Of great energy and sensing the need of new buildings he designed the Church of The Sacred Heart, the first of this dedication in this country. He supplied the money for the work by the sale of his ancestral estates in France and from the pension paid yearly by France due to the wounds he sustained in battle.

This church was designed with columns and pedestals in the classic of the period. Above the altar is a Painting of Martha and Mary given by King Charles the tenth and a painting of The Sacred Heart given by a Maryland lady.

Other necessary buildings were designed and built at the convent which has become well known as a school for girls. He died September 29, 1826 and was buried at the Convent.

JOSEPH F. COCKERILL was born in 1864 in Port Richmond, S. I. and studied at Cooper Union in the Department of Architecture. He was a member of the A.I.A. and the societies of architects in Staten Island and New York. Died June 17, 1942.

ALFRED I. COFFEY was born in San Francisco in 1886 and was graduated from Saint Mary's College. He specialized in the design of hospitals and was the architect of the Southern Pacific Hospital; the Harkness Memorial; Saint Francis; the Cancer unit and Pyschopathic Building of the City Hospital; and a number of public schools. For a period he was City Architect of San Francisco. Died Nov. 10, 1931.

CARROLL COLETTI was born in 1905 and was graduated from the Quincy High School in Quincy, Massachusetts. He received the degree in architecture at Yale University. He was finalist in the American Academy in Rome competition of 1930; winner of the Inter-collegiate Collaborative Competition in 1930; won the Rotch Travelling Scholarship in Europe for two years which is the oldest architectural scholarship in America.

He was Chairman of the Board of Education at the Boston Architectural Center and taught advanced design there. He was a painter in water color and belonged to the Boston Society of Water Color Painters and had exhibited at many places in New England.

With his brother Paul he was the architect of many buildings in the vicinity of Boston including the Don Orione Rest Home, Chapel and Infirmary; the Remington Rand Office Building in Boston; additions to the Thomas Crane Public Library in Quincy; the Administration Building at Quincy City Hospital; many public schools.

Registered in Massachusetts and with the National Board of Registration he was one of the charter members of the Massachusetts Association of Architects; a director for three terms and President in 1957. A member of the A.I.A. and of the Massachusetts Commission of Fine Arts; the Yale Club of Boston and President of L'Eco. Died 1957.

PLATE X. Music Hall, Boys Town, Nebraska. Leo Daly, Architect. (Photograph by Walter S. Craig.)

33

JOHN THEODORE COMES was born at La Rochette in Luxembourg, Jan. 29, 1876. His father was an artist specializing in church wood carving. When his son was eight years old he was brought to this country and settled in Saint Paul, Minn. Here the son attended school until entering Mount Saint Mary's College in Emmitsburgh, Md. Later the college conferred the degree of Master of Science in Architecture upon him.

In 1897 he came to Pittsburgh and during his life there he designed more than fifty buildings in the diocese. Some of the buildings were the churches of Saint John the Baptist in Liberty Avenue in 1907; The Holy Family in Latrobe; Saint Gertrude in Vandergrift in 1912. The same year Saint Paul in Butler; Saint Paul's Cathedral School; a Retreat House; the Monastery for the Redemptorist Fathers; the Church of Saint Agnes in Cleveland and the Cathedral in Toledo, Ohio. His most important work and the finest it is thought is the Church of Saint Luke in Saint Paul, Minn. This is built of Indiana limestone with tiled roof; shallow transepts and the interior walls banded in light and dark stone, as in the Cathedral of Siena, and a ceiling of tile. This was completed after his death.

He was the founder of the Pittsburgh Architectural Club; a member of the City Art Commission; the City Planning Board; Knights of Columbus; Society of Saint Vincent de Paul and the Catholic Truth Society. Author of many articles upon church architecture. Died April 13, 1922.

JAMES F. CONNELL was born in 1869 at Port Richmond, Staten Island, N. Y. and was a student in architecture at Cooper Institute. He designed the Church of The Resurrection in Manhattan and the Church of Saints Peter and Paul in Mount Vernon; a number of theatres in New York City such as the Rivoli, Ambassador and Adelphi and others in Buffalo. He was a director of Cooper Union; a member of the A.I.A. and the Staten Island Society of Architects.

JOHN F. CONNELL was born in Delavan, Ill. August 4, 1899. He studied at the Colorado Agricultural and Mining College from 1918 to 1920. He was graduated from Notre Dame in 1923. He travelled much in Europe, North Africa, Asia Minor and Central America. In practice in Denver, Colo. he was the architect of Saint Peter and Saint Paul School in Wheatridge, Colo., Saint Augustine School in Brighton, Colo. and Saint Pius Tenth Church and Hall in Aurora, Colo. Member of the A.I.A. Died in 1957.

LEON COQUARD was born in Detroit, September 27, 1860 and practiced there. He was architect for Saint Mary's Church and the Academy of Saints Peter and Paul; the Cathedrals of The Immaculate Conception in Denver and Saint Mary in Covington, Ky. Died in 1926.

FRANCISCO CORREJOLLES was of Spanish descent and worked in New Orleans during the early part of the nineteenth century. Among his designs is the Beauregard House in New Orleans built in 1826. He died November 11, 1835.

GABRIEL CORREJOLLES, a brother of Francois and his associate, died Oct. 11, 1842.

ANGELO M. CORRUBIA was born in Italy and was brought to this country as a child when his parents settled in Saint Louis. He was educated at Washington University in Saint Louis; the University of Illinois and was graduated from Massachusetts Institute of Technology.

PLATE XI. St. Louis Hotel, New Orleans, Louisiana. J. N. B. Pouilly, Architect. (Photograph courtesy of the New Orleans Public Library Archives Dept.)

At the University of Illinois he taught in the Department of Architecture and established an office in Saint Louis where he practiced for a number of years. He was the architect for important buildings including the Convent of The Sacred Heart; the Charles Duncker, Jr. Memorial Hall at Washington University and as an associate on the Clinton-Peabody Terrace housing project. He was the founder of Scarab, the national architectural fraternity and its president; founded the Business Mens' Art Club of Saint Louis; member of the board of the Saint Louis Artists' Guild. He was also a landscape painter. Died Dec. 9, 1943.

PAUL PHILLIPE CRET was born in Lyons, France October 23, 1876, the son of Paul Adolphe and Anne Caroline Cret. He received his early education at Saint Bonaventure's School in Lyons; the Lycee of Bourg and the School of Fine Arts in Lyons. He received there the Paris Prize for study at the Ecole des Beaux Arts in Paris. In 1901 he won the Rougevin Prize and was a gold medalist of the Salon of 1903. The same year he received the Diploma of the French Government.

In 1903 he was appointed Professor of Design at the University of Pennsylvania, a position he held until 1937 when he became emeritus professor. In association with Albert Kelsey he received the commission, as a result of a competition, for the Pan American Building in Washington. This building, the first to be built from his designs, shows the remarkable and careful attention to all details that characterized his work. Afterwards with Zantziger, Borie and Medary he was architect of the Public Library in Indianapolis; The Federal Reserve Bank in Philadelphia; the War Memorials in France; the Rodin Museum in Philadelphia and the Academic Building and Gymnasium at West Point were products of his office.

Many honors were received such as the degree of Doctor of Science from the University of Pennsylvania in 1913; the Master of Arts degree from Brown University in 1929; the Doctor of Arts degree from Harvard in 1940. He was given the Bok Prize as an outstanding citizen of Philadelphia; a Fellow of the A.I.A.; member of the Philadelphia Jury; a member of the Federal Fine Arts Commission; member of the Commission on the Chicago Fair of 1933; member of the American Battle Monuments Commission and Chevalier of the Legion of Honor. Died September 8, 1945.

HYACINTHE LACLOTTE was a partner of Latour and a pupil at the same academy in Paris. He volunteered as a private with Jackson and later was on Jackson's staff. He established a school for architects and taught construction when the school was at Orleans and Royal Streets. He designed the house of Dr. Mourises in New Orleans.

V. G. LA MAISTRE was at one time an architect in New Orleans.

FATHER JUAN CRESPI was born in Mallorca in 1721. He came to Mexico and then was a missionary in Sierra Gorda where he built a stone church in Valle del Filaco. Died at San Carlos Mission, Jan. 1, 1782.

RICHARD CROSE was born May 14, 1896 at Towanda, Ill. He spent most of his life in Chicago and died in South Bend, Ind. in 1958.

PLATE XII. Saint Patrick's Seminary, Menlo Park, California. Charles H. Devlin, Architect.

ARTHUR F. CROWLEY was born in Yonkers and was educated at the City College of New York. He was associated with the firm of Voorhees, Foley and Smith. Died Sept. 26, 1947.

FATHER ANTONIO CRUZADO was born near Alcarazegos near Cordova in 1725 and came to Mexico in 1748. He worked for twenty-two years as a missionary of Sierra Gorda and then came to San Gabriel where he spent thirty-three years. Died October 12, 1804.

CORNELIUS CURTIN was born in Louisville, Ky. March 20, 1853 the son of a professor who came from Dublin, Ireland to teach in Louisville. He was trained in Louisville offices and was the architect for the Columbia Building in 1890 which was one of the early fireproof buildings of the city; architect of the City Hall annex and Saint Bridget's Church. A member of the A.I.A. Died January 17, 1926.

PHILIP ALAIN CUSACHS was born in New Orleans of French ancestry in 1888. He was educated at Tulane University and later studied at the Ecole des Beaux Arts in Paris. Until 1930 he was associated with his brother-in-law R. T. Almirall in Brooklyn and was prominently connected with the Beaux Arts Institute of Design. He was the architect for a number of large estates in the southern states. Died August 1, 1931.

HENRY D. DAGIT was born in Philadelphia in 1865 and was educated in the public schools and trained in local offices. Later he worked for W. H. Geissenger and became an associate in his office.

In 1888 he opened his own office which he maintained for thirty years until joined by his sons, Henry, Alfred and Charles who have continued the practice. He was appointed in 1908 as the architect for the Diocese of Trenton and held the position for ten years. For that diocese and in Philadelphia he designed many churches and schools.

In 1908 he designed the Church of Saint Francis de Sales which is notable for its great dome of Guastavino construction. He was architect for the Archbishop's House and supervised the restoration of the Cathedral. Among his other works are the high school of The Little Flower; the Church of Saint Catherine of Siena and the church of Saint Edward both in Baltimore; the Monastery at Villanova, Pa.; Rosemont College Chapel and the Cathedral in Atlanta, Ga. Died March 25, 1929.

LEO A. DALY was born in Omaha, Neb. in 1890 and spent his life there. He attended Creighton Preparatory School from which he was graduated and also from Creighton University. He was well and favorably known for his work and that of his firm which he founded and conducted for thirty-five years.

He was architect for the Omaha Municipal Stadium; the World Herald Building and the Memorial Building in the World War Two Memorial Park. In Saint Louis the firm designed the Jesuit Philosophy Institute and in the suburbs of Omaha the buildings for Boys' Town which he regarded as his masterpiece. Died August 6, 1952.

ZACHARY TAYLOR DAVIS was born in 1872 and he was associated with his brother in much commercial work and apartment houses. He was architect of the Court House in Kankankee, Ill., Saint Ambrose Church in Chicago where his funeral was later held. With Gustave Steinbach he was architect of the Quigley Seminary in Chicago whose chapel is one of the notable ecclesiastical buildings in the

PLATE XIII. Holy Cross Church, Holyoke, Massachusetts. John William Donahue, Architect.

city. In later years he was Superintendent of repairs for the Chicago Board of Education and also designed many baseball parks throughout the Middle West. Died Dec. 16, 1946.

FATHER FRANCIS XAVIER DE COEN, was born in Flanders about 1811. He was a priest of the Society of Jesus and came to America where he taught for several years at Bardstown, Kentucky and later was in the Diocese of Leavenworth, Kansas. He is credited with the design of the Cathedral and its resemblence to that at Bardstown may have been caused by his residence in the former town. He was described by the Bishop as a good architect and administrator. He was nephew of Father Charles Nerinckx, a native of Belgium, who founded in Kentucky the Sisters of Loretto in Kentucky at the beginning of the 19th century. Father De Coen also did much missionary work among the Pottawatomi Indians of Kansas.

AUGUSTUS DE GRASSE as he was listed in Charleston, S. C. was Alexander Francois Augustus, Marquis de Grasse, a son of the Admiral de Grasse who fought for the American cause in the Revolution as Commander of the French Fleet. After the death of the Admiral and the outbreak of the French Revolution the family took refuge in Haiti from which it was necessary to come to the United States after the revolution began in that island. On August 14, 1793 the de Grasse family arrived in Charleston after a voyage of seventeen days from Cap Francois the former name of Cap Haitian. The family consisted of the widow of the Admiral, her son, the Marquis, and four daughters. Two of the latter were married later in Charleston and the two younger ones died there due to an epidemic and were buried in Saint Mary's churchyard. Later the Marquis had his two daughters baptized in the same church and for a period he was an architect in the city. In June 1800 he advertised a school of design but when conditions became more stable he returned to France.

LEO DEILMANN was born in San Antonio, August 14, 1881. He was graduated from Saint Mary's College in San Antonio in 1898 and then studied at the Technical Institute at Idstein, Germany until 1901.

Returning to his native city he was a building inspector for three years, and alderman and a member of the Library Board. He belonged to the K. of C.; the Catholic State League of Texas, the Sons of Herman; Alhambra and the A.I.A.

ANDREW L. DELEHANTY was born in Albany, N. Y. in 1888 and was graduated in architecture at Carnegie Institute of Technology. He was the architect for many parish and public schools in Albany and among these were the Philip Livingston Junior High School and the church of Saint Theresa, rectory and school. Died Nov. 19, 1943.

MATTHEW WILLIAM DEL GAUDIO was born in Italy, March 16, 1889 the son of Gabriele and Rebecca Palermo Del Gaudio. He was brought to the United States in 1892 and later studied at Cooper Union, the Mechanics Institute and at Columbia. He did much work in apartment design, churches and public building.

He was prominent in professional societies being a past president of the New York Society of Architects of New York City; the New York State Association of Architects; chairman of the Joint Commission of Architectural Societies of the Metropolitan Area Director of the A.I.A.

PLATE XIV. Auditorium, Oakland, California. John Donavan, Architect. (Photograph by Albert Harris & Associates.)

He served in both world wars becoming a major. He was Bronx County commander of the American Legion; past Commander of United Bronx Post 17. Also chairman of the legislative commission of Bronx County Grand Jurors Association.

He received the Gano Dunn Medal for professional achievement from the Cooper Union Alumni Association. A Fellow of the A.I.A. Died September 18, 1960.

CHARLES H. DEVLIN was born in San Francisco in 1858 and with his brother formed a firm that did much Catholic work. Among these were additions to Saint Ignatius church which at the time of its building was considered the largest steel framed structure west of Chicago. Another important building was Saint Patrick's Seminary at San Mateo. His death occurred September 12, 1928.

His brother Leo who had been his associate died in 1933.

JOHN HENRY DEVEREAUX was born in Waterford, Ireland July 26, 1840 and he was brought to America in 1843 when his family settled in Charleston, S. C. His interest at first seemed to be sculpture and when a young man he modelled the bust of Preston S. Brooks.

At twenty he was a captain of cavalry and inspector of depots for the War Department of The Confederate States. After the war he acted as an architect for the Treasury Department of the United States. He worked mostly in Charleston and in 1867 was architect for Saint Matthew's Lutheran church and in later years the Academy of Music and the Masonic Hall.

His summer home was on Sullivan's Island and here he was active in the building of the Church of Stella Maris. Both he and the priest in charge worked upon the foundations of the building. He died March 16, 1920.

ARTHUR DILLON was born in Saint Louis in 1870. He was a descendent of August Choteau who was one of the founders of the city. His father was John Dillon who had established a notable position as an editor before he was brought to New York by Joseph Pulitzer to head the New York World. His son came with him and was educated at Phillips Academy at Exeter, N. H. and he was graduated from Massachusetts Institute of Technology and the Ecole des Beaux Arts in Paris.

He formed the once prominent firm of Dillon, McClellan and Beadle. He was architect for a number of monuments and memorials including the War Memorial at Lake Champlain and the library at South Orange, N. J. He was a consultant for the Essex Park Commission and a member of The Architectural League of New York and the Beaux Arts Society. Died June 6, 1937.

ANTONIO DI NARDO was born in Italy, Feb. 1, 1889 at Pennapeid, Monte Chieti. He was brought to the United States by his parents in 1895 and studied at the University of Pennsylvania. He won the Stewardson Scholarship and studied in Europe before he entered Philadelphia offices.

Later he taught at Western Reserve University in Cleveland an established an office in that city. He designed a number of parish schools and churches there and in Detroit. He was well known for his water colors. Died June 6, 1925.

JOHN WILLIAM DONAHUE was born in Springfield, Massachusetts in 1869, the son of Florence and Mary Welch Donahue. His father was connected with the engineering department of the Boston and

PLATE XV. Connecticut College for Women, New London, Connecticut. Ewing & Chappell, Architects.

Albany Railroad and designed the large office building for the railroad in Springfield. The son was educated in the schools of the city including the Central High School and later worked in offices of local architects.

Later he became the architect for the Diocese of Springfield and in that position which he held for the rest of his life he designed many Catholic buildings. In Springfield he designed the churches of Our Lady of Hope; The Holy Family; All Souls; Mount Carmel; Our Lady of The Sacred Heart High School; Holy Cross Church in Holyoke, Mass.; Saint Brigid's in Amherst, Mass.; Saint Anne in West Springfield; Saint Bernard's in Worcester, Mass; Saint Luke in Pittsfield. The new buildings for the College of Our Lady of the Elms and the Mother House of the Sisters of Providence. In Rhode Island he was architect for La Salle Academy. A member of the A.I.A. Died March 5, 1941.

JOHN DONAVAN was born in North Andover, Mass. March 25, 1875. He studied at Phillips Academy in Andover, Mass. and was graduated from Massachusetts Institute of Technology.

He worked on the Singer Building in New York which was designed by Ernest Flagg and in Pittsburgh where he was employed by Palmer and Hornbostle. The latter firm sent him to supervise the work on the City Hall in Oakland, California. There he remained the rest of his life.

He was the architect of the City Auditorium, many public buildings and schools in Oakland; for Saint Mary's College and for Santa Clara University. He was one of the consulting architects for the Oakland Bridge and author of a book upon school buildings which was regarded as an authority on the subject.

He was president of the Northern California Chapter of the A.I.A. and a member of the State Board of Examiners for Architects. Died March 20, 1948.

JOHN DORAN in 1834 designed the church of Saint Joseph at Sixth Avenue and Washington Place, in New York City.

JOHN F. DRANEY was born March 17, 1880 in Poughkeepsie, N. Y. where he attended Saint Peter's School and the Riverview Military Academy. He was graduated from Pratt Institute in Brooklyn, N. Y.

For many years he was associated with William J. Beardsley in Poughkeepsie who was a prominent architect in that city. Later he was architect for many religious and educational buildings. Among these were Holy Trinity church in Arlington; Saint Christopher's in Red Hook, N. Y. and the churches in Goshen and Marlboro, N. Y. In Poughkeepsie he was architect for the Infirmary; the Elks and the Knights of Columbus buildings.

A member of the Fourth Degree of the Knights of Columbus; the Elks; Dutchess County Society; Friendly Sons of Saint Patrick; Society of Architects of New York State; Holy Name Society. Died March 25, 1938.

ADOLPH DRUIDING was an architect in Chicago who devoted himself largely to the design of Catholic churches in the mid-west, during the early decades of the 20th century. He published a book showing some of his work and among these designs is the Church of Saints Peter and Paul in Pittsburgh, Pa.

PLATE XVI. Rockefeller Center, New York City. Harrison & Fouillhoux, Architects. (Photograph by Thomas Airviews. Courtesy of Rockefeller Center, Inc.)

FATHER DUBUIS was born in France in 1817 and came to work in the Texas missions where because of limited means he was the architect and builder of a number of early churches. His first church was of stone which he quarried and dressed. The same procedure was followed at Castroville and at San Antonio.

In 1862 he was consecrated a bishop in France and returned to that country in 1881 and died in 1896.

FATHER FRANCISCO DUMETZ was a native of Mallorca and came to San Gabriel Mission in California where he died Jan. 14, 1811.

EDWIN F. DURANG was born in 1825 and practiced for many years in Philadelphia. Later he was joined by his son F. Ferdinand Durang and together they did many churches and institutional buildings in Pennsylvania and New Jersey. Among the buildings in Philadelphia are the Gesu Church and the Church of Our Lady of Mercy. Died June 12, 1911.

JOHN JOSEPH EARLY was born in New York City, Dec. 18, 1881 and he studied at Saint John's College from 1894 to 1899. Later he worked in Washington and was greatly interested in the use of color in his work. He worked on the copy of the Parthenon built in Nashville, Tenn.; the BaHa'i Temple in Wilmette, Ill. and the Shrine of The Sacred Heart in Chevy Chase, Maryland.

VINCENT J. ECK was born in Williamsport, Pa. of a family long established there and he received his elementary training in the city before entering Notre Dame where he was graduated in architecture in 1915. He was the architect for four Bishops of Trenton and did many schools and other Diocesan work until his death May 20, 1938.

JAMES J. EGAN was born in Cork, Ireland, the son of William and Mary Fitzgerald Egan. He was educated at a private academy in Cork and at the Government School of Design at Queen's College in Cork. He studied in England before coming to New York where he worked for several years in offices including that of Potter and Upjohn. He went to Chicago after the fire of 1871 and remained. He was the architect of the Criminal Court Building and received the commission to design the County Court House.

In 1897 he became a partner of Charles H. Prindeville and the firm did many churches and institutions. In Chicago: the Church of Saint Elizabeth; the Church of The Holy Angels; Saint Xavier's College and Saint Vincent's College. Hotels such as the Brevort in Chicago; the Ryan in Saint Paul and the Spaulding in Duluth. In San Francisco the Church of Saint Mary survived the earthquake of 1906. One of the last buildings of the firm was the Cathedral of Saint Paul in Pittsburgh. A member of the A.I.A. Died Dec. 2, 1914.

WILLIAM P. ELLIOT was born at the beginning of the 19th century and was a pupil of George Hadfield in Washington during the building of the City Hall. Three years were spent in study in Europe principally in London and Paris. He was appointed soon after to design the Patent Building. Questions arose regarding his age and he associated himself with Ithiel Town. The work later, as so often happens, was given over to another architect although Elliot's designs were retained. He died in Washington,

PLATE XVII. City Hall, Baltimore, Maryland. George A. Fredericks, Architect. (Reproduced from the Collections of the Library of Congress.)

Nov. 3, 1954 and his funeral services were at Saint Patrick's Church of which Hoban was one of its chief supporters.

HENRY ENGELBERT was in practice in New York City for a number of years. He was the architect for Holy Cross Church on W. 42nd Street and for Saint Gabriel's.

ALEXANDER C. ESCHWEILER was born in Boston, Mass. in 1865. His mother was a member of the Chadbourne family, one of the oldest in Maine and in New England. His father was a German mining engineer. The family moved to the copper country of Michigan where schooling opportunities were sparse. Later the family settled in Milwaukee and the son attended Marquette University. He studied at Cornell where he was graduated in 1870. He was employed for a number of years in Milwaukee offices before beginning his own practice. Later his three sons who had in turn followed his educational experiences at Marquette and Cornell joined him in his office.

The firm established a reputation for distinguished work so that any design coming from that office was sure to be of superior quality. Some of the buildings designed there are the church of Saint Rose in Racine, Wis.; the church of Saint Thomas Aquinas in Milwaukee; the Plymouth Congregational Church in Milwaukee; the First Universalist church in Wausau; the House of the Good Shepherd; Downer College; the Law Building and Science Building all in Milwaukee; Redemptorist Monastery and a Cistercian Monastery both in Oconomowoc, Wis.; many commercial buildings and buildings for the Wisconsin Telephone Company. Died 1940.

FATHER LUKAS ETLIN, O.S.B. in association with Conradi of Saint Louis designed the Chapel of Perpetual Adoration in Clyde, Mo. and other buildings. Died Dec. 16, 1927.

CHARLES EWING who was a grandson of Thomas Ewing, once Secretary of the Interior, was educated at Georgetown University and later practiced in New York City with George S. Chappell. One of their important commissions was the design of the first buildings for the Connecticut College for Women in New London. These buildings were marked by great skill and did not copy simply medieval forms but were given a distinctive character. Later in association with Jerome Allen he was architect for some large buildings in New York such as the Architects' Building in Park Avenue and the Science Building at Vassar College. Died Nov. 24, 1954.

VINCENT F. FAGAN was born in Hopedale, Mass. in 1898 and was educated in the parish schools of the town. In 1920 he received a degree in architecture at Notre Dame. For a brief period he was employed in a Boston office and then was appointed to the staff of the Department of Architecture at Notre Dame. He was associated on some of the buildings at Notre Dame and with Cram and Ferguson on the Dining Hall. Later in independent practice in South Bend he was architect of All Saint church in Hammond, Ind. and Saint Matthew's School in South Bend. Died in July, 1951.

CHARLES FANTONI was in practice in San Francisco for a number of years during which time he was architect for the Church of Saints Peter and Paul and in Watsonville, California for the Church of Our Lady, Help of Christians. A member of the K. of C.; the Swiss Relief Society and the Italian Catholic Federation. Died June 20, 1933.

PLATE XVIII. Court House, Amarillo, Texas. Townes and Funk, Architects.

CHARLES ALLEN FAVROT was born in 1866 in Baton Rouge, La. He studied there and was graduated from the State University of Louisiana in 1884. For a period he worked for James Freret and then attended Cornell University. He began his own practice in 1890 and later was associated with Louis Adolphe Livaudais for thirty-seven years.

The firm designed many important buildings and among these were the Roosevelt Hotel and the Hutchinson Memorial at Tulane University. Member of the A.I.A. and Chairman of the City Planning and Zoning Commission. Died March 10, 1930.

FRANCIS STILLMAN FISH was born in 1886. He studied at Saint Ignatius College in Cleveland, Columbia University and the Ecole des Beaux Arts in Paris. He was associated with E.T.P. Graham on work in Cleveland and during the First World War he was Director of Construction for the Knights of Columbus War Activity. He was a member of the Cleveland Chamber of Commerce; the K. of C.; Cleveland Art Museum; Beaux Arts Society of Architects. Died June 14, 1957.

WALTER F. FONTAINE was born in 1871 in Fitchburg, Mass. He studied in Europe and worked in Providence offices until he opened his own office in Woonsocket. He was architect for Saint Mary's Church in Willimantic, Conn.; Saint Charles Borromeo Church in Providence and Saint Joseph's College in Fitchburg. Died 1938.

JOSEPH T. FORTIN was born in 1870 and came to Chicago from Canada at the age of nineteen. He studied architecture there and also was graduated from the Kent College of Law in Chicago. He was a founder of the Illinois Society of Architects and maintained his own office for many years. He died while waiting for Mass at the Church of Notre Dame in Chicago, Jan. 25, 1956.

JOHN J. FOLEY was born in San Francisco April 4, 1882. He studied and was employed in his native city and also studied at Armour Institute in Chicago. In the latter city he worked for Weber, a prominent designer of business buildings, and then later returned to the Pacific coast.

He was employed at this time by prominent architects in San Francisco and was licensed to practice in the state in 1913. His work extended throughout Northern and Central California and is largely ecclesiastical. Among these designs in San Francisco are Saint Joseph's church; Holy Name church, school and rectory; Star of the Sea convent and school; St. Mary's Catholic Hospital; In Winnemucca, Nevada the church of Saint Paul.

He was a member and Grand Knight of K. of C.; a member of the Fourth Degree; Holy Name Society and the League of The Cross. He died with his wife in an automobile accident in Los Angeles April 20, 1946.

JACQUES ANDRE FOUILHOUX was born in Paris, France, Sept. 27, 1879 the son of Jean Baptiste and Leonie d'Echeverry Fouilhoux. He was educated at the Lycee Janson de Sailly in Paris; received the A. B. and B. S. degrees at The Sorbonne and the civil and mechanical engineering degrees at the Ecole Centrale et Manufactures. In 1904 he came to the United States and worked for Albert Kahn and later went to Portland, Ore. There he formed the partnership of Whitehouse and Fouilhoux that lasted from 1908 until 1914.

PLATE XIX. Mission of St. Xavier del Bac, Tuscon, Arizona. Ignacio Gaona, Architect. (Reproduced from the Collections of the Library of Congress.)

51

In 1913 he had become a citizen and in World War I he joined the army as a member of the 129th Artillery and fought at St. Mihiel, the Meuse and in the Argonne battles. He was made a major and received the award of the Legion of Honor. Returning to this country he was associated with Raymond Hood in the competition for The Tribune Building in Chicago and their design received first prize. Later the firm designed the American Radiator Building in New York; the Daily News Building and with Frederick Hirons the McGraw-Hill Building.

With Walter Harrison he designed the Trylon and Perisphere at the New York World's Fair which set the distinctive tone to the Exposition. Then with Harrison and Abramovitz the firm designed such buildings as those of Rockefeller Center and the Clinton Hill development.

He was Treasurer of the Beaux Arts Institute of Design; President of the New York Building Congress; a Director of the French Hospital in New York; member of the Board of the Catholic Protectory; the K. of C.; prominent in the work of the Society of Saint Vincent de Paul. He was a member of professional societies such as the A.I.A.; the American Society of C. E.; American Society of Heating and Ventilating Engineers and the Architectural League. His death on June 20, 1945 was caused by a fall from the scaffolding while inspecting work.

GEORGE ALOYSIUS FREDERICK was born in Baltimore, Md. on Dec. 16, 1842, the son of John M. and Margaret Frederick. He was educated by the Christian Brothers and in 1858 was a pupil in the Office of Lind and Murdoch.

He entered a competition for the new city hall of Baltimore and won first prize although not twenty-one at the time. The Civil War intervened and the building was not completed until 1875. It was erected within the appropriation and two hundred thousand dollars were returned to the city. He was employed on architectural work at Druid Hill and other public parks and was the architect of the U. S. Marine Hospital; Saint Joseph's Hospital; Baltimore City Hospital; Whiteford Hall; many residences; the churches of Saint Pius, Saint Theresa, Saint James and Holy Cross in Baltimore. At Annapolis he designed Saint Mary's Hall and renovations at the State House. He was a Fellow of the A.I.A. and served many terms as a director. Died August 17, 1924.

JAMES FRERET was born in New Orleans April 26, 1838, one of nineteen children of James P. Freret. He studied at Spring Hill College in Mobile and later in Paris. Freret Street near Loyola College in New Orleans is named for his family. Joining the army of the South he began his practice after the war and did a number of important buildings among them being Saint Patrick's Hall; the Louisiana Sugar Exchange and the Produce Exchange. At Spring Hill College he worked with Claude Beroujon on the main building after the destruction by fire of the earlier building. He is considered one of the founding benefactors of Spring Hill due to his generous contributions to its establishment. Died Dec. 11, 1897.

WILLIAM FRERET was born Jan. 19, 1833 a cousin of James Freret and son of the Mayor of New Orleans, William Freret, who died in 1864.

He was educated at Spring Hill College and at Baton Rouge and later went to Paris for study. At the outbreak of war between the North and South he joined the forces of the Confederacy. Later he opened an office in New Orleans. He was in the office of the Supervising Architect of the U. S. Treasury and was Engineer for the State of Louisiana. After the burning of the State Capitol in Baton Rouge he restored

PLATE XX. French Opera House, New Orleans, Louisiana. James Gallier, Jr., Architect. (Reproduced from the Collections of the Library of Congress.)

that building and designed the House of Charity and some of the buildings for the State University. Died June 25, 1881 in New Orleans where his funeral was held from the Church of Notre Dame.

ALDEN FREEMAN was born in Cleveland, Ohio May 25, 1862, the son of Joel F. and Frances M. Abbey Freeman. He received the B. S. degree from New York University in 1882 and the M. S. degree in 1887. He was associated with Lorenzo B. Wheeler for a brief period. He organized the Citizens Union of East Orange, N. J. for political reform and was Chairman of the Franklin Mansion at Perth Amboy, N. J. For a number of years he was consul general for Haiti in Miami.

In World War I his home was given as a convalescent hospital and took care of one thousand soldiers from 1918 until 1921. He was donor of Elmwood Park Playground in East Orange and the Montarioso Memorial Park in Santa Clara, Cal.

He was an honorary member of the V.F.W.; the Society of Colonial Wars; Sons of the Revolution; Phi Beta Kappa; Society of Cincinnati; Red Cross Society of Japan; Society of Mayflower Descendents; New York Yacht Club; Metropolitan Club; Jockey and Housekeepers Clubs. He was a contributor to reviews on political reform; author of Year in Politics; Forerunners of Woodrow Wilson; Abbey Memorial of Enfield, Conn. Died March 15, 1942.

G. RABEY FUNK was born in Savannah, Ga. Nov. 10, 1903. He was graduated from the high school in Tucumcari, N. M. where his father, Godfrey, was a builder for many years. Rabey Funk was graduated from the University of Notre Dame in architecture. He went to Amarillo where he soon became known as one of the leading architects of West Texas. His firm of Townes and Funk designed a number of large public buildings such as court houses and churches in West Texas and eastern New Mexico. The Court House in Amarillo and the one in Raton, N. M. and his last work the ward buildings at the state hospital in Big Springs. He did much for the Church during his brief life. This fact was attested to by the honor paid to him at his funeral Mass at which the Bishop of Amarillo preached in the presence of the Archbishop of Santa Fe. He was a member of the K. of C. and was district deputy Grand Knight of the Panhandle. He organized the fourth degree, was long a member of social and civic organizations and a member of the Texas Association of Architects. Died Dec. 12, 1939.

FREDERICK BOWEN GAENSLER was born in San Antonio, Texas in 1879. He studied at Saint Mary's College conducted by the Brothers of Mary in San Antonio. For a time he worked in local offices and then entered Massachusetts Institute of Technology. After completing the course in architecture he was employed by T. P. Chandler in Philadelphia until he returned to his native city to open an office.

He was architect for many churches and schools in southwest Texas. Among these are the college Building of the Sisters of The Incarnate Word; the chapel at the convent of The Incarnate Word; Saint Mary's Church for the Oblate Fathers. He was a charter member of the Architectural Society of San Antonio. Died Jan. 27, 1941.

IGNACIO GAONA had the direction of building the Mission of Saint Xavier del Bac at Tuscon, Arizona. The Mission had originally been founded by Father Eusebio Francisco Kino in 1692 but it was not until the latter part of the 18th century that the present church was built. Gaona was a Spanish

PLATE XXI. Battle Monument, Baltimore, Maryland. Maxmilian Godefroy, Architect. (Reproduced from the Collections of the Library of Congress.)

architect and his assistant was Pedro Bajourquez. Gaona fell from the tower which has remained un-completed since his death. As late as 1937 his descendents were living in the adjoining state of Senora where he had built the sister mission of Concepcion at Caborca similar in style and proportion to San Xavier.

JAMES GALLIER, JR. was born in 1827 the son of James Gallier who had been trained in England and Ireland. The younger Gallier was early in his father's office and associated with him in much of his work such as the French Opera House and the Pontalba Buildings. The interior of Saint Patrick's Church is considered to be his design as he was a pew owner in this church. Died 1868.

HERMAN GAUL was born in Horrem, Germany July 30, 1869. His early education was obtained in his native country and in 1886 he came to the United States. At first in Saint Paul he worked in offices until 1891 and then returned to Germany and entered the University in Holzmunden where he received the degree of Master Builder in 1894 which is regarded as the equivalent of an architectural degree in this country. Having returned to the United States he opened an office in 1902 having been licensed to practice in Illinois. Later he was joined by his sons. He had an extensive practice in the mid west and designed such notable structures as Holy Hill in Wisconsin; the Josephinum in Chicago; hospitals such as Saint Elizabeth's, Chicago; Good Counsel Sanitarium, Mankato, Minn.; Saint Francis, Evanston, Ill.; Saint Anne's, Chicago; Angel Guardian Orphanage, Chicago. Many monasteries and mother-houses such as The Precious Blood, Carthagena, Ohio; The Society of The Divine Word, Girard, Pa.; the Poor Hand Maids, Donaldson, Ind. Died Nov. 24, 1949.

CHARLES ANTOINE COLOMB GENGEMBRE was born in Paris in 1790. He joined the Corps de Garde of the King of Westphalia. In 1809 he built the Mint in Cassel, France and in 1814 he competed and won second place in the competition for the Grande Prix de Rome. Later with others he travelled in Italy.

In 1820–1825 he was making designs for illumination of the Grand Opera by means of oleaginous gas and in 1826 he designed the Porte St. Ouen in Paris. When King Louis Phillipe came to the throne the work was abandoned. He left France and went to London in 1831. He had patents for six-wheel loco-motives and made plans for the Manchester and Liverpool Railroad.

In 1841 he was appointed to build dredging machines and he was architect for communal schools. At the fall of the King in 1848 he left France and came to Cincinnati and a year later to Manchester, Allegheny City, Pa. His family became well known. Since the surname was difficult for Americans to pro-nounce the children adopted the surname of Hubert the family name of their mother. One of the sons, Philip Hubert, became well known as an architect for apartments in New York and Los Angeles. From 1862 to 1864 the father was the architect for the new City Hall of Allegheny which was not completed at his death.

LEWIS C. GIELE. Saint Augustine Church in New York on 167th Street and the Sacred Heart Hospital in Allentown, Pa. were designed by him.

56   RAYMOND GLEESON was born in Philadelphia in 1899. He received the degree in 1921 in architec-

PLATE XXII. Saint Lawrence Church, Asheville, North Carolina. Rafael Guastavino, Architect. (Photograph by June Glenn, Jr.)

ture at the University of Pennsylvania and he worked principally in his native city. He was associated with the firm of Gleeson and Mulrooney. He was a member of the Philopatrian Club; Cahill Club; the A.I.A. and was a director of the Roman Catholic High School for Boys. Died Feb. 3, 1958.

MAXMILIAN GODEFROY was born in the latter part of the 18th century in France. He served in the King's Guard and was a captain of cavalry. He had grown up at the time when Ledoux was designing custom houses and other public buildings where mass and proportion were emphasized. In 1805 he came to Baltimore to teach architecture, military engineering and drawing at the College of Baltimore which later became Saint Mary's Seminary.

In 1807 he designed the Seminary chapel which is considered to be the first Gothic Revival design in the United States. Later with Benjamin Latrobe he designed the Baltimore Exchange. He was the architect of the Commerce and Farmers' Bank in Baltimore; the First Presbyterian Church; the Unitarian Church and in 1816 the Court House in Richmond, Va. He made a design for a triumphal arch for Baltimore and was the architect for the Battle Monument which still stands although in surroundings that have changed greatly in the course of time.

He designed the fortifications for the city in 1814 which resisted the attacks of the British on September 20th of that year.

He had married Mrs. Anderson, a widow, who was well known as one of the first women editors in this country. She had been born in England but was reared in America. Conditions grew unpleasant for them here and they returned to France where he was appointed architect for the Department of Mayenne. During their residence in Laval, Mrs. Godefroy, who had become a Catholic, died Oct. 2, 1839 and soon after he left France for England where he had previously spent a number of years. His later years remain unrecorded.

JOHN STAFFORD GROMELIN was born in Washington, D. C. Oct. 7, 1895. He studied at the University College School in London and University College, London. He received the degree of A. B. from Princeton and studied at Georgetown University.

At the Ecole des Beaux Arts in Paris he received the Diploma of the French Government. He was a member of Phi Beta Kappa. During World War I he was a captain in the U. S. Army. Later he was with Holabird and Root of Chicago. A member of the A.I.A. and president of the Chicago Chapter. Director of the Chicago Building Congress. Died April 2, 1957.

RAFAEL GUASTAVINO was born in Valencia, Spain, one of fourteen children. He was reared by his uncle in Barcelona and about 1880 he came to this country with one of his sons. He had been trained as an engineer and architect and had developed a system of vault construction which he had used in smaller buildings in Spain. He considered that the opportunities in this country for this system would be greater. The architects here were beginning to design large structures that they wished to be fireproof and from this period on the Guastavino system of vaults was used. At the World's Fair in Chicago in 1893 he designed the Spanish Building. He first came to Ashville, N. C. as consulting architect for Biltmore House in 1889. He contributed his services and part of the funds for the construction of Saint Lawrence Church. This has an elliptical dome 82 by 58 feet. The terra cotta figures were by him. The high altar was designed by Stanford White and the reredos is of carved walnut from an old Spanish church. Later in

58

PLATE XXIII. Dubuque County Court House, Dubuque, Iowa. Fridolin Heer, Architect.

1909 White designed the Lady Chapel which serves as the burial place of Guastavino. At Wilmington, N. C. he designed Saint Mary's Church and this was supervised by Rafael Guastavino, Jr. The interior walls are of mosaic. He is considered one of the notable benefactors of The Church in North Carolina. He was a musician and composer of many compositions that have been published. Died 1907.

RAFAEL GUASTAVINO, the second, was born in Barcelona and came with his parents to New York in 1881. He was largely trained by his father and engaged in much important work. It was his firm that built the great dome of Saint John the Divine in New York; the work at the State Capitol in Nebraska; Saint Thomas P. E. Church and Saint Bartholomew's in New York. He also invented the manufactured sound absorbing stone used in the construction of the Riverside Church in New York and elsewhere. A member of The Architectural League of New York and the Ceramics Society of America. Died October 18, 1947.

DOUGLAS FRANCIS HALEY of Gary, Indiana was born in 1931 and lived most of his life in Gary. Educated and received his degree in architecture from the University of Notre Dame. Designed a number of public schools in the Calumet area as well as churches. A director of the Gary Chamber of Commerce; member of the Indiana Society of Architects and of the A.I.A.; president of the Board of Directors of the Smith Industries for the Blind. Died Jan. 23, 1960.

GEORGE EDWARD HAYNES was born in Boston in 1875 where he received his architectural training. At the age of twenty-six he went to Pittsfield, Mass. where he remained the rest of his life. He was employed as an architect by the General Electric Company for several years. The year he came to the city he won first place in a competition for the Mercer School and after that a large number of business structures were designed by him such as the Miller Building; apartment houses; the Crane and Hibberd schools; the Church of Mount Carmel. In Worcester he designed the Church of All Angels; in Chicopee the High School; in Westfield the Mosely School. In Pittsfield he was architect for the Father Matthew Total Abstainance Society Building of which he was president and director. He was a member of the National Academy of Social and Political Science; a Fourth degree member of the K. of C. During his later years his daughter who had been graduated from New Rochelle College and the Department of Architecture of M.I.T. was associated with him in his practice. Died Oct. 27, 1932.

JOHN HAYNES was born in Saint Louis, March 1, 1861. He was educated in the public schools and worked as a draughtsman. Later he became Deputy Commissioner of Saint Louis County Building Commission and then joined the firm of Barnett and Barnett. The firm of Barnett, Haynes and Barnett did much important work throughout the Midwest. Among their buildings are the Jefferson Hotel; Post Dispatch Building; Star Building; Marquette Hotel and the Mark Twain Hotel in Hannibal, Mo. In Chicago the Illinois Athletic Club. The new Cathedral of Saint Louis is the outstanding work of the firm. Died Oct. 30, 1942.

LEO J. HEENAN was born in Jackson, Michigan August 1, 1890. Later his family brought him to Pontiac where he was reared. A graduate of the local high school he was trained in the offices of the architects there and later established an office. He was architect for a number of buildings such as the

PLATE XXIV. Cathedral of St. John The Divine, New York City. Heins & Lafarge, Architects.

City Hall; the Public Safety Building; the General Hospital; the Adah Shelly Branch Library; the Childrens' Home; County Infirmary and a number of schools. He was a city assessor for three years, chairman of the Pontiac Historical Commission, the County Board of Supervisors, the Michigan Society of Architects, the Illuminating Engineering Society, the A.I.A., Rotary Club, City Club. Died October 20, 1957.

FRIDOLIN HEER was born in the Canton of Saint Gall, Switzerland March 31, 1834. His father was a builder and the son was apprenticed to a carpenter but in his leisure time studied architecture. He became a builder and in 1864 came to the United States. He settled first in Belleville, Ill. and then went to Chicago but left there for Dubuque, Ia. Here he remained and became well known in Iowa and Wisconsin. Among his designs were the Church of The Sacred Heart; Saint Francis Convent and Orphans' Home in Dubuque; the Sacred Heart Church in Madison, Wis.; the Church of Saint Anthony in Milwaukee; the original buildings for Saint Mary's Academy in Prairie du Chien, Wis. and the Dubuque County Court House. A Fellow of the A.I.A. Died March 9, 1910.

FRIDOLIN HEER, JR. was born in Chur, Switzerland Sept. 9, 1864 and shortly after was brought to this country. He was educated in the public and parish schools and worked for Adler and Sullivan in Chicago. From 1881 to 1883 he was a student at Campion College in Prairie du Chien, Wis. After graduation he went to the Royal Architectural School in Stuttgart, Germany. When he returned he joined his father and they designed the parish school of The Sacred Heart and the Auditorium in Dubuque; Saint Mary of the Angels Home for Young Women; Saint Joseph's Academy; Saint Columbkille parish school; work at Saint Mary's Orphans' Home; the Fulton and Irving public schools; churches at Fort Madison, Ia; Pomeroy, Ohio; Duersville, Ill. From 1886 until 1940 the buildings at Saint Mary's Academy in Prairie du Chien. A Fellow of the A.I.A. Died Mar. 1, 1940.

GEORGE L. HEINS was born in Philadelphia May 4, 1860. He attended the public schools and was graduated from Massachusetts Institute of Technology. He worked in offices in Minneapolis and Saint Paul and in 1886 associated with Grant La Farge in entering a competition for the Church of Saint John the Divine to be built in New York City. There were twenty-five competitors and in the second stage four. The commission was given to Heins and La Farge. It is interesting to note that the two largest Protestant churches being built in the first half of the twentieth century—Liverpool in England and Saint John in New York—were designed by three very young Catholic architects: Scott and Heins and La Farge, and both as a result of a competition. For twenty years the work continued as the money became available until the death of Mr. Heins. At his death the trustees revoked the contract and the work was given to another architect.

During their association many commissions were received: The Church of The Blessed Sacrament in Providence, R. I.; Saint Paul's Church in Rochester, N. Y.; Church of The Good Shepherd, Shelton, Conn.; Saint Michel's chapel and parish house in New York; the Catholic chapel at West Point; Saint Matthew's Church in Washington, D. C. which is now the Cathedral of the Archdiocese of Washington.

In 1889 he was appointed State Architect by Governor Theodore Roosevelt. He was a Fellow of the A.I.A. and died September 25, 1907. At Lake Mohegan, N. Y. Saint George's Church was built by Mrs. Heins in his memory.

PLATE XXV. National Gallery of Art, Washington, D. C. Eggers and Higgins, Architects. (Photograph courtesy of the National Gallery of Art.)

JOSEPH I. HIGGINS was born in Berkeley, R. I. and spent most of his life in Fall River, Mass. where he practiced his profession as an architect of schools and churches. Included in these are the Monsignor Coyle High School in Taunton, Mass. He was a member and trustee of Saint Patrick's church in Fall River and a counselor for the Catholic Youth Organization and greatly interested in the athletic activities of the city. Died Oct. 8, 1940.

WILLIAM B. HELMKAMP was born in Fort Jennings, Ohio in 1886. After his earlier schooling there he was graduated in architecture at Notre Dame in 1911. He began work in Akron, Ohio and then formed a partnership with Robert Kraus. Their practice was extensive and among their buildings were Saint Thomas Hospital; Ayer Hall, Knight Hall and the Physical Education Building at the University of Akron; Saint Sebastian Church and parish buildings; Saint Peter's Church and Saint Augustine's School in Barberton, Ohio. Died August 26, 1953.

DANIEL PAUL HIGGINS was born in 1886 in Elizabeth, N. J. He studied by correspondence at the Alexander Hamilton Institute Business College and worked as a bricklayer. Later he studied at New York University. For many years he was associated with John Russell Pope and at the death of Mr. Pope, he, with Otto Eggers, continued the practice under the name of Eggers and Higgins.

His architectural work was large and important such as the Alfred Smith Memorial at Saint Vincent's Hospital in New York; the American Red Cross Building; the Senate Office Building; The National Gallery of Art; Aetna Life Building; interiors of the Grace Line ships.

He was active in many civic organizations; eight years a member of the Board of Education in New York City; Chairman of the Committee on Buildings and Sites; Chairman of the Board of Catholic Youth Organizations; member of the Madison Square Boys' Club; The Boy Scouts. He received the Gold Medal of the Architectural League of New York; the award given by Cardinal Spellman for Catholic Youth Organization and was created a Knight of Malta. Died Dec. 27, 1953.

WILLIAM E. HIGGINS died in San Jose California in 1936.

FRANCIS GEORGE HIMPLER was born near Treves, Germany in 1833, the son of Leonard and Christine Hasbron Himpler. He studied architecture for four years at the Royal Academy of Arts in Berlin and travelled in Europe for a period. He established a reputation there and in Vaudrevange in Lorraine he designed a church.

In 1867 he came to Atchinson, Kansas where he designed and supervised the erection of the Benedictine Abbey. Then he moved to Hoboken, N. J. and later to New York City. In Hoboken he was the architect of the Academy of The Sacred Heart and the Church of Our Lady of Grace; in Saint Louis the Church of Saints Peter and Paul; Saint Francis de Sales Church in Cincinnati; Saint Anne's Church in Buffalo, N.Y. and in New York City the Church of Saint Alphonsus. He was architect of the City Hall in Hoboken. He paid much attention to the acoustics of the large auditoria that he designed. He was keenly interested in numismatics and belonged to the Numismatic Society of New York. His interests covered archeology, botany, geology and mineralogy. In 1906 he published a book: *The Beauties of Lake Hoptacong* dealing with the flora of that district. He died there Sept. 13, 1916.

64

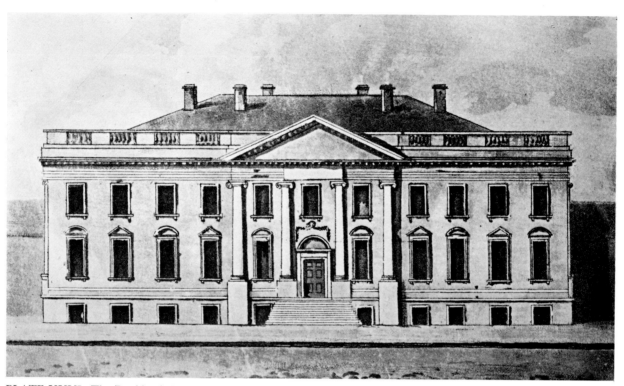

PLATE XXVI. The President's House, Washington, D. C. James Hoban, Architect. (Reproduced from the Collections of the Library of Congress.)

JAMES HOBAN was born about 1762 in Callan, County Kilkenny, Ireland, the son of Edward and Martha Bayne Hoban. He studied in the schools of The Dublin Society where the classes were taught by Thomas Ivory who died in 1782 and who had been the architect of a number of important buildings in Ireland. On Nov. 23, 1780 several boys were considered to receive medals and Hoban was given the second premium for his drawings of brackets and stairs. He worked on the Royal Exchange in Dublin and in 1781 on the Custom House. Shortly after this he was in Philadelphia for on May 25th, 1785 he advertized in a paper there. In 1792 he was in South Carolina and designed the Capitol in Columbia. In 1791 he was mentioned in The Charleston Post and Daily Advertizer as architect of a theatre. He took part in the competition for the building of the Federal City and his design for the President's House received first premium which was a building lot in the city and five hundred dollars. Later he was retained to supervise the construction of it for a fee of three hundred guineas. On Sept. 13, 1793 he was at the laying of the corner stone and continued in charge until the building was occupied. He was the only one who had remained continuously identified with the buildings of the new city for his knowledge, abilities and probity were always respected. In the city he designed the Great Hotel from 1793 until 1795 and the Little Hotel in 1795.

He had been first introduced to the Commissioners of the Federal City by General Washington who stated that he had been strongly recommended to him by Col. Laurens, a gentleman of South Carolina. Hoban was appointed as an associate of Dr. William Thornton and was to supervise the construction of the new capitol building. He laid the foundations of the building in 1815 after several sets of contractors had defrauded the Government. He resigned in 1795 but at the request of the Commissioners he returned to the work in 1798 and stayed until the appointment of Latrobe who was to be Surveyor of Public Buildings in 1803.

It is interesting to note the influence of Catholics in the early building of the new city. In 1804 Latrobe tried to have Canova come to this country to work and although he was sympathetic he could not as he was working for the Duke of Tuscany. He obtained the best man available instead, his kinsman, Giuseppe Franzoni who was his assistant. The latter came the next year with many servants, several painters and sculptors and among them Giovanni Andrei. Franzoni was a man of great cultivation and dined with the President at the President's House several times a week. For ten years he worked on the enrichment of the new buildings. Nothing remains of his work as it was destroyed in the fire set by the British in the invasion of the capital. Six months after the fire he died and was buried in old Saint Patrick's Cemetery. His brother Carlo came the next year with Francesco Isadello as an assistant. Carlo had been employed by Pope Pius the seventh and to these Italian artists the corn capitals of the north vestibule are probably due and of which Anthony Trollope mentions as "the only original thought noted in America."

All these Italians as well as Hoban and L'Enfant were members of Saint Patrick's parish. The climate was hard on these Italians and caused the death of most of them as it had of the Irish who had come from the south to Washington. However, they were there long enough to start a band to relieve their homesickness and they trained some Americans to play and from this developed the Marine Band.

Highly thought of by Washington, Hoban was a captain in the Washington Artillery Company and led his command to escort Washington on his return from Philadelphia to Mount Vernon. In 1799 he was elected to the City Council and remained a member until his death. He designed the first State and War Offices in 1818.

67

PLATE XXVII. Mission of San Jose, San Antonio, Texas. Pedro Huizar, Architect. (Reproduced from the Collections of the Library of Congress.)

In January 1799 he was married to Miss Susannah Sewell who belonged to the noted Massachusetts family and from this marriage ten children were born. He was always on friendly terms with the other architects and superintendents who were working in Washington and he was noted for his generous character and hospitality. He died Dec. 8, 1831.

ARTHUR HORGAN was born in 1848 and died September 12, 1912.

RAYMOND F. HOULIHAN of Chicago practiced there until his death. At the time of his death he was vice-president of the Illinois Society of Architects.

THOMAS HOUGHTON was born in Brooklyn in 1840 and was educated in the schools of that city. During the Civil War he was paymaster in the United States Navy. He was trained in the office of Patrick C. Keely whose oldest daughter he married. After the death of Keely he was the architect of a number of churches such as Holy Family chapel at Convent, N. J.; the churches of Our Lady of Victory and Saint Francis Xavier in Brooklyn and a number of churches in Boston and other New England cities. Died Dec. 6, 1903.

JOSEPH C. HUBER was born in 1884 and was graduated in architecture from Columbia University. He was appointed diocesan architect of Toledo by Bishop Schrembs. During this time he did much work upon schools and churches. He was associated for a period on the work of the new Cathedral. Among his designs are the Monastery of The Visitation and Saint Stephen's church in Toledo. Later he was architect for the Government at the Kingsbury Ordnance Plant in Indiana. While employed there he died in La Porte, Indiana on July 23, 1954. A member of the A.I.A.

PROSPER L. E. HUERNE was born in France Nov. 11, 1860 where he was educated in engineering at Chalons. When he was thirty he came to California and settled in San Francisco where his ability was soon recognized.
Work of magnitude came to him such as the work on the docks and the street railways. At the time of his death an obituary stated that he had also been connected with the early work on the Panama Canal. He was the architect for the French Hospital and the church at the Mission. Died October 5, 1892.

PEDRO HUIZAR whose name is associated with several of the missions about San Antonio, Texas was born in the Canary Islands. He came first to Mexico and then to Texas. He was employed to survey and draw plans for the Presidio of Nuestra de Loreto. He gave an estimate also for the cost of irrigating the lands of the Mission.
In 1793 he surveyed for the distribution of the land belonging to San Antonio de Valero (Alamo). He received title to a tract of farmland. He did the same work for the Mission of San Francisco de la Espada on July 12 and July 16 for the Mission of San Jose de Aguayo. He was given title to the granary which his family held for 116 years. In 1798 he was married to Gertrude Martinez in the Cathedral of San Fernando but she lived only for a brief time. Later he was building the Mission church at San Jose and while there met one of the girls who sang in the choir and for whom he had a great admiration. According to the tradition her death occurred while he was starting to carve the noted window and he devoted this to her memory.

69

PLATE XXVIII. Detailed view of the Mission of San Jose. Pedro Huizar, Architect. (Reproduced from the Collections of the Library of Congress.)

RAPHAEL HUME was an architect who for many years devoted himself to liturgical art in The Church. He was born in New York in 1889. Among his designs are the Church of Saint John and Saint Mary at Chappaqua, N. Y.; the chapel at Canterbury School in New Milford, Conn.; Saint Joseph's Hospital in New York; the Public Library in Scarsdale, N. Y.; plans for the reconstruction of the University of Nijmegan in The Netherlands; He was a member of the A.I.A.; the Municipal Art Society of New York; the Architectural League of New York; president of The Liturgical Arts Society and the Charter Commission of Stamford, Conn. He was created a Knight of Saint Gregory in 1948. He died while on vacation in Mexico City, Feb. 15, 1957.

CHARLES F. HUMMEL was born in Garnsbach, Baden, April 12, 1857 and came to the United States in 1887. He settled in Boise, Idaho in 1894 where he practiced until his death. Among the buildings he was architect for are the Eastman Building; the Hotel Boise; the Senior and Junior High Schools; Saint John's Cathedral and with John Tourtellote the Capitol of Idaho. A member of the Idaho Historical Society. Died Sept. 17, 1939.

WILLIAM P. HUTCHINS was a native of Pittsburgh and was reared in the parish of Saint John the Baptist. He attended the University of Pennsylvania and opened an office in Pittsburgh. He designed a number of churches in this Diocese such as Saint Francis Xavier; Saint John's in Uniontown; Saint James in Wilkensburg; Saint Brendan in Braddock. His last work was the Memorial Hall built at Toner Institute as a memorial to Father Sigmund. He designed many churches for missionary districts and which were built by the aid of The Church Extension Society of Chicago which depended in many cases upon the generous contribution of designs by Mr. Hutchins. Died in 1942.

JOSEPH ICARD was living in New York at the beginning of the 19th century and was described as an "eminent architect." He was successful enough to be able to suscribe twenty thousand dollars for national defense in this country. His office was later closed and he returned to France when that country became more tranquil and there he amassed a fortune in Paris. His will was probated July 7, 1817 with his nephew as administrator.

WILLIAM O'DONNELL ISELIN was born in 1883 and was graduated from Harvard cum laude in 1905. He then was graduated from Columbia and the Beaux Arts in Paris. Later he served as a lieutenant in the Navy and was associated with the office of Warren and Wetmore.

JOSEPH JACOBBERGER was born March 19, 1868 in Alsace Lorraine and was brought to this country when a child. He was educated at Creighton University in Omaha, Nebraska and for a short period he was settled in Minneapolis.

In 1912 he went to Portland, Oregon where he did much Catholic work. He was the architect for Saint Clement's School of Nursing; the Chapel of All Saints' Church, Maryhurst College and the Cathedral of Saint Mary in Portland; the House of The Good Shepherd; the Church of The Madeleine; the University of Portland Campus Plan and the K. of C. Club House. A past president of the Oregon Chapter of the A.I.A. Died March 18, 1930.

PLATE XXIX. State Capitol, Boise, Idaho. Tourtellote and Hummel, Architects. (Photograph by Johnson A. Boise. Reproduced from the Collections of the Library of Congress.

JOSEPH JAHAN was born Sept. 1758 in Montargis, France and then came to Santo Domingo but in 1793 he took refuge in Charleston, S. C. where he worked as an architect and builder. He was a member of the Societe Francais and a vestryman at Saint Mary's Church. Died Jan. 30, 1833.

JOURNOT, an architect in New Orleans, built in 1836 a house in Barracks Street but little is known of other work.

THEODORE KAUTZKY was born in Budapest on October 20th, 1896. He was a graduate of the Royal University of Hungary in 1821. He came to America in 1923 and six years later was naturalized.

He devoted himself largely to making presentation drawings for various architects and taught at Pratt Institute, New York University, University of Pennsylvania and the University of Toronto. He won the Birch Burdette Long Prize for his work in delineation and wrote a number of books upon drawing and architectural illustration. In the international competition for the building of The Chicago Tribune he received honorable mention. Died 1953.

CHARLES S. KEEFE was born in 1876 in Kingston, N. Y. and was educated there. After many years in New York City he returned to Kingston and designed a number of buildings there. Among these were the American Legion Building; the Knights of Columbus Building; Wadsworth Museum in Hanover, N. H.; the restoration of the Crane Museum at Dalton, Mass. He edited a revised edition of The Georgian Period in this Country and wrote numerous articles upon architectural subjects. He was architect for a number of small houses. A former President of the Mid Hudson Valley Architectural Society and a member of the A.I.A. Died July 19, 1946.

PATRICK CHARLES KEELY was born in Thurles, County Kilkenny, Ireland in 1816. He received his early education locally and worked with his father who was a successful builder in Kilkenny where he built the College that still stands in that city.

In 1842 he came to Brooklyn, N. Y. and began work as a carpenter. In a short time he had an opportunity to design a church which when built was considered as outstanding at a period when churches were rare on Long Island. After that there were many commissions that came to him from all over the country east of the Mississippi River. From New Orleans to Montreal are to be found examples of his work. He did nearly all the churches and institutions of the Dominicans and many of the Jesuits as well as those for secular parishes. His work developed and some of his churches show remarkable construction and a variety of treatment even though he is credited with having designed more than six hundred churches. Many of these were to be cathedrals at the time or later. The Cathedral of The Holy Cross in Boston is one of the largest covering nearly an acre and the Cathedral of Charleston, S. C. is one of the most interesting and has been little changed since its building. The cathedrals of the five New England states were by him and many of the parish churches are still standing. In Watertown, Wis. is the most northerly of those in the United States. The Cathedral of Hartford, Conn. was supervised by his son Charles who had been trained in his father's office—the only one to follow the father's profession. A promising career was ended when he died of pneumonia at the Bishop's House where he was a guest while the Cathedral was under construction.

The second time that the Laetare Medal of the University of Notre Dame was conferred it was awarded to Keely for his outstanding work. Active until his death which occurred in the summer of 1896.

PLATE XXX. Cathedral, Portland, Oregon. Joseph Jacobberger, Architect. (Photograph by Photo-Art Commercial Studios.)

WILLIAM KEELEY was a native of County Tipperary, Ireland and at one time lived in Pittsburgh, Pa. He is considered to be the architect for the Custom House in Erie, Pa. which was once the U.S. Bank of Pennsylvania and an outstanding example of Greek Revival architecture. He later went to Louisville, Ky. where he designed the Cathedral of The Assumption; the Abbey Church of Gethsemani and the chapel of Saint Vincent de Paul for the Sisters of Charity at Nazareth, Ky. He lived later in Peewee Valley where he was one of the trustees.

JOHN FRANCIS KELLY was born June 17, 1875 in New York City. He studied at the Passaic High School in New Jersey, Pratt Institute in Brooklyn and the Massachusetts Institute of Technology. He was Business Manager of the Board of Education in Passaic.

In that city he designed many public and private buildings and also in northern New Jersey. Some of these were the Passaic High School; Passaic National Bank and Trust Company; Passaic Police Building; Junior high schools One, Eleven, and Twelve and public schools Eight and Nine; K. of C. Building and Saint Nicholas Parish School. He had been an outstanding athlete and was an authority upon Oriental rugs. He was a member of the K. of C.; the A.I.A.; the New Jersey Planning Board; Scholarship Committee of M.I.T. Died in Passaic Oct. 23, 1940.

JAMES KENNY was an architect and builder in Charleston, S. C. and built there the Orphans' Home for Boys of which Barbot was the architect. In 1867 he was architect for the Academy of Mercy in Sumter, S. C. later known as Saint Joseph's Academy.

HENRY J. KEOUGH was born in Richfield Springs, N. Y. Jan. 1, 1884. He was graduated in architecture at Syracuse University in 1909. Later he went to Detroit and was in the firm of Van Leyen, Schilling and Keough. The firm was architect of the South West High School in Detroit, Saint Thomas Church; the Fordson High School in Dearborn, Mich.; Mercy Hospital in Muskegan, Mich.; the churches of Saint Theresa, Saint Thomas and Saint Gregory.

He was a member of the Board of Directors and Treasurer of the Michigan Society of Architects; the A.I.A.; the Michigan Engineering Society and for four terms the President of Sigma Chi fraternity alumni. He died in 1957 and was buried in Saint John's Cemetery in Worcester, Mass.

PIERRE IVES KERALUM—"El Santo Padre Pedrito" as he was called by his people—was born on March 2, 1817 in Quimper, Brittany. He was first trained as a cabinet maker and then as an architect. When he was twenty eight he decided to study for the priesthood and entered the diocesan seminary in Quimper. He became an Oblate in 1851 and volunteered to go to the missions in Texas. At Roma his early training came to his aid for here he designed a small church acting as the architect, stone cutter and mason.

Earlier in his life in Texas he designed the church of The Immaculate Conception in Brownsville which is of brick Gothic design. The chandeliers were secured from France and the church was for that period a great addition to the work of the missionaries.

Later he was at Mercedes. Here he worked among the poor and it is related that a non-Catholic seeing him going along the road with a number of boards on his shoulder followed from curiosity to see what the priest was doing. He found him in the house of one of his parishioners who had died and the priest was fashioning a coffin for the man.

PLATE XXXI. Cathedral of the Holy Cross, Boston, Massachusetts. Patrick C. Keely, Architect. (Photograph by J. H. Buffords.)

75

His health began to fail and his eyesight also but he persisted in doing his work. In November 1872 he started on horseback to visit the outlying parishioners. After a few days the horse returned without its rider or saddle. Search was made but no trace of the priest was found. Ten years later some cowboys searching for cattle found the shreds of a saddle hanging on a tree and at the foot of the tree some human bones that gave evidence of being gnawed by animals, a chalice and other articles of a priest's equipment and about twenty dollars. The latter showed it was not robbery that caused his death but these relics were removed and deposited in the church he had designed in Brownsville.

JOHN H. KERBY was born in 1858 in New York City and studied at Cooper Union and Fordham University. He was architect of Saint Martin of Tours Church; Saint Thomas Aquinas Church and Saint John's Hall at Fordham. He attained the military rank of colonel. Died August 4, 1936.

J. PETER KLINGES was born in Philadelphia and was graduated from the University of Pennsylvania in 1906. He worked for a number of years there until his death October 8, 1918.

EDMUND J. KNIGHT was born November 8, 1908 and was graduated from the University of Notre Dame with a degree in architecture. He was associated with several firms largely in supervising construction in Guam, Panama and the United States. Died December 15, 1960. A member of the A.I.A.

ROBERT V. KNOX was born in Crystal Lake, Ill. and was graduated from the Department of Architecture at Notre Dame in 1927. He spent several years in Springfield, Ill. and then came to Saint Joseph, Mich. where he had an office. He served in the U.S. Navy as a lieutenant and was badly injured. He resumed practice at the end of the war and built many churches and schools in southern Michigan. Among these were churches in Three Oaks; Bridgman; schools in South Haven; in Saint Joseph, Saint Joseph's School and in Benton Harbor, Saint John's School. At Berrien Springs, Mich., he designed several of the buildings at Emmanuel College. He was a member of the Elks; the Michigan Society of Architects; Berrien County Country Club and the Disabled American Veterans. He died in a London hospital while on a Holy Year pilgrimage to Rome, Nov. 25, 1950.

THEODORE KOCH was born in Scranton, Pa. July 1, 1886. He was trained in the office of Lewis Handcock in Scranton and later became a partner. He travelled in Europe studying church architecture in Italy, France and Germany.

In the Scranton office such churches were built as Saint Mary's at Priceburg, Pa.; Saint John the Baptist in Scranton.

At the oubreak of World War I he was sent by the Federal Government to Newport News, Va. for a course in shipbuilding and then was assigned to the Staten Island Shipyard. He also served with the Bureau of Biological Survey supervising construction in their program. For a long time he was employed by McKim, Mead and White and acted as supervising architect for many projects such as Bellevue Hospital in New York and in Burlington, Vermont at the University of Vermont. During World War II he was again employed at the Staten Island Shipyards. Later he was associated with Maurice Uslin until his death March 23, 1957. A member of the A.I.A.

PLATE XXXII. Public Library, Salt Lake City, Utah. C. Grant LaFarge, Architect. (Photograph by Deseret News Photo.)

EDWARD LA BELLE was born in Montreal in 1867 and was educated in Stuttgart, Germany. Upon his return he practiced many years in Chicago and died in Oak Park, Ill. September 17, 1942.

ARSENE LACARRIERE LATOUR was the principal engineer for General Jackson in 1815. He had graduated at the Academy of Fine Arts in Paris and in New Orleans he wrote a history of the war in West Florida and Louisiana. He was the architect for the house of the Le Monnier family on Royal Street; the first Orleans Street Theatre; the Rogers house on Bourbon Street. Henry Latrobe and Latour designed the house of Jean B. Thierry who was the editor of Le Courier in 1814.

HYACINTHE LACLOTTE was a partner of Latour and was a graduate of the same school in Paris. He volunteered as a private with Jackson and later was a member of Jackson's staff. He with Latour established a school for architects where he taught construction. He was the architect of the house of Dr. Mourises and the Monnier house at Royal and Saint Peter Streets and the "New Theatre."

GEORGE LAFAYE was a native of New Orleans and a student at the Jesuit College. Later he practiced in South Carolina where he died May 11, 1939.

CHRISTOPHER GRANT LA FARGE was born in Newport, R. I. Jan. 5, 1862, the son of John La Farge and Margaret Perry. He was a grandson of Christopher Grant and Frances Sergeant Perry and Jean Frederic de la Farge; a great grandson of Commodore Oliver Hazard and Elizabeth Champlin Mason Perry and through Frances Sergeant, a descendent of Benjamin Franklin and John Dickinson. His father was distinguished as a painter and designer who taught his son to draw. From 1880 to 1881 he was at M.I.T. and then went into the office of H. H. Richardson. Here he formed a friendship with George L. Heins and was in Minneapolis with him until they returned in 1884 to New York where he took care of the architectural work of his father.

In 1885 the two young architects became partners in the competition for the great church of Saint John the Divine and also did some commercial work in the West. Out of a large list of competitors four were selected for final consideration and of these four the design of Heins and La Farge was given first place and the commission to build was awarded to them. This work occupied their attention for twenty years until the death of Mr. Heins. Then it was assumed that the work would continue in the firm but on Mr. La Farge's return from Europe he learned that the trustees had terminated the contract and given the work to another architect.

Later a partnership was formed with Benjamin Wistar Morris and during this period and later when alone much work was done such as the Cathedral of Saint James in Seattle, Wash.; secular buildings as the Naval Hospital at Brooklyn, N. Y.; stations of the New York subway; buildings at the Zoological Park; the Public Library at Salt Lake City, Utah; the Williams Memorial at Trinity College, Hartford, Conn.; the New York City Genealogical Society Building.

He was a former President of the N. Y. Chapter of the A.I.A.; of the Architectural League; a member of the National Board of Directors of the A.I.A. and a vice-President; member of the Committee on Education of the A.I.A.; Chairman of the Advisory Committee of the School of Architecture at Columbia and M.I.T.; Fellow of the A.I.A. Died Oct. 11, 1938.

PLATE XXXIII. Cathedral of Saint Peter, Detroit, Michigan. F. Letourneau, Architect. (Reproduced from the Collections of the Library of Congress.)

CHRISTOPHER GRANT LAFARGE was born Dec. 10, 1897, the son of C. Grant LaFarge. He was graduated from Groton School in 1916 and received the degree of A. B. from Harvard in 1920 and the degree of B. S. in Architecture in 1923 from the University of Pennsylvania. He was employed with McKim, Mead and White and then by Ware and Clark before entering his father's firm of LaFarge and Son. He exhibited water colors in several galleries before giving up the practice of architecture in 1932. For the rest of his life he devoted himself to writing. Died 1955.

EDWARD L. LARKIN was born in 1887. With his brother John A. Larkin he was well known as an engineer and architect. Before the depression the two brothers as the head of a corporation had planned a 110 story building for offices which was to be built on West 42nd Street in New York and which site is now occupied by the McGraw-Hill Building. He was architect for many apartment houses and commercial buildings among them being the Printing Crafts Building in Eighth Avenue at 34th Street.

He was well known for his work for the needy being for six years the president of the Particular Council of Saint Vincent de Paul Society; a trustee of Saint Bernard's Church in West Fourteenth Street and president of Saint Bernard Conference; chairman of a committee of the Saint Vincent de Paul camp for poor children at Spring Valley, N. Y. He was created a Knight of Malta for his fifty years of work in charity. Died 1959 from a fall sustained while supervising the construction of an apartment house in Brooklyn,

FATHER FERMIN FRANCISCO DE LASUER, a native of Victoria Alava came to California in 1768 where he died June 26, 1803. A great builder and administrator of the Missions.

JOSEPH LA VEILLE came to Saint Louis in 1821 from Harrisburg, Pa. and with George Morton, a native of Edinburgh, formed the first architectural firm west of the Mississippi River. They were the architects of the first Episcopal church in that section. In 1834 they completed the Catholic Cathedral. They built the court house with a semi-circular portico on the square set aside for the purpose by Auguste Choteau and J. B. Lucas. In 1826 the first buildings at Jefferson Barracks were built. From 1823 to 1826 La Veille was a street commissioner and alderman of the south ward. He died in 1842 and it is assumed his grave is in Saint Vincent's Cemetery since it is in that ward that he lived.

FRANCIS LETOURNEAU was for many years an architect in Detroit and with Father Kinderkins designed the Church of Saint Peter in 1841 for the Jesuits.

LA RICHE an architect in New Orleans active in 1824.

EUGENE LETANG was born at Boulleret in the Province of Berri, France in 1842. He was a student in the Atelier Vaudremer and after winning the Grand Prix de Rome he studied there before he was invited to come to Boston to teach at the Massachusetts Institute of Technology. Here he was a distinguished teacher of design for twenty-two years but did not engage in outside work. A bronze tablet to his memory was placed in the Fine Arts Library of the Boston Public Library. At the time of his death Professor William Ware who had brought him to this country wrote a tribute in *The American Architect* as follows: "Thoroughly trained in his calling, skillful and experienced in construction and design. No one could

PLATE XXXIV. Academy of Music, Philadelphia, Pennsylvania. N. LeBrun, Architect. (Photograph courtesy of The Historical Society of Pennsylvania.)

work with him or under him without being fortified and stimulated in his moral nature and being made ashamed of trifling and half hearted endeavors. He believed in the importance of his work and would tolerate no trifling in his pupils. He was one in a thousand." Died in Boston in 1892.

NAPOLEON EUGENE HENRY CHARLES LE BRUN was born in Philadelphia Jan. 2, 1821, the son of Charles and Adelaide Le Brun. His father had come to America on a secret diplomatic mission to President Jefferson and then returned later to live permanently in this country. He was the son of Louise Alexandrine de Manduit and Sir Charles Pierre Eugene Le Brun. The mother of Napoleon Le Brun was Adelaide Louise Marie de Monignon Madelaine and the daughter of Marie de Monignon and Leonard Madelaine. On their way to Louisiana in December 1791 the parents of Mrs. Le Brun came to Philadelphia and the father died of yellow fever in 1793. Leonard Madelaine was a coach cypher maker at the time of his death and his wife lived until 1817. The father of Napoleon Le Brun was teaching and translating in 1814 and his wife had an academy for young ladies. Napoleon, who was named for the Emperor, was well educated in the classics.

He showed an aptitude for art and engineering and was sent to study with Thomas U. Walters who had been a pupil of William Strickland who in turn had been with Benjamin Latrobe. In that way the architectural ancestry of young Le Brun gave him the best possible training that was available at that time in America. His family ancestry was also noteworthy: his uncle was Thomas Antoine, Chevalier de Manduit Plessis who came to America at his own expense with Lafayette. He was a lieutenant in the artillery and fought at the battle of Red Bank where he was captured by Count Dunop. Later he was killed by the revolutionists in Santo Domingo in 1791. Napoleon Le Brun at twenty opened his own office and among his first designs was the German Catholic Church of Saint Peter at Fifth Street and Girard Avenue. The corner stone was laid in 1843 and the building was completed in 1845. In the crypt is the body of the Venerable Bishop Neumann. At the time of its completion the church was considered one of the most distinguished and dignified in the city.

He enlarged the Jefferson Medical College and was the architect of the Seventh Presbyterian Church; the Church of The Nativity; the Scots Presbyterian Church and the Academy of Music. The latter now having passed its centennial year is still highly regarded for its design and for the superior qualities of the auditorium. The interior of the Cathedral of Saints Peter and Paul was his work and the former Church of Saint Patrick. The latter has since been replaced by one designed by Heins and LaFarge.

At the end of the Civil War Le Brun went to New York to establish his office there where he and his sons did large work. One building is the Church of Saint Elizabeth at 187th Street and Broadway. This is distinguished by the aid given by such notable citizens as Joseph Fisher and James Gordon Bennett who gave the ground; Charles O'Connor who gave ten thousand dollars, Mr. Bennett five thousand and Mr. Fisher two thousand. The high altar was the gift of Miss Fisher and Mr. Bennett gave a copy by May of Murillo's painting of The Immaculate Conception. The Church of The Epiphany of Our Lord at Second Avenue and 22nd Street seating over sixteen hundred and modelled after the Church of Saint Zeno at Verona; the Masonic Temple; the Foundling Asylum; the new City Hall; the Hall of Education; the Home Life Building and from 1889 to 1909 the Metropolitan Life Building in Madison Square. The latter was an experiment in tall buildings in the use of columns in the construction. It received the award of the New York Chapter of the A.I.A. in 1909 as the most meritorius of the year.

He was a member of the Board of Trustees of the A.I.A. and a Fellow; a member of the Board of

PLATE XXXV. Metropolitan Tower, New York City. N. LeBrun & Sons, Architects. (Photograph by Irving Underhill. Reproduced from the Collections of the Library of Congress.)

83

Examiners to the New York Building Department and President of the Williard Architectural Commission for forming a collection of architectural models at the Metropolitan Museum. Died July 9, 1901.

PIERRE LE BRUN, the son of Napoleon, who worked with his father was born in 1846 and died Feb. 14, 1924. He founded the Le Brun Travelling Scholarship and was the founder of the Art Library at Montclair, N. J.

MICHEL MORACIN LE BRUN was born in 1856 and died Oct. 4, 1913. He with his brother carried on the traditions of the work of their father and both were members of the A.I.A.

PIERRE CHARLES L'ENFANT was born in Paris Aug. 2, 1754. His father, Pierre, was a painter in ordinary to the king in the Manufactory of the Gobelins. His paintings are to be seen in the Musee de Versailles. The mother was Marie Charlotte Leuiller. He had instruction in engineering and architecture but at the age of twenty-three he came to this country at his own expense to fight as a volunteer for the colonists. He spent freely of his modest means for American independence. He was brevetted as a lieutenant in the French colonial forces and through Congressional resolutions received a commission as first lieutenant of engineers with rank from Dec. 1, 1776.

He sailed Feb. 14, 1777 from L'Orient with Col. du Coudray, a month ahead of Lafayette and spent the winter at Valley Forge. In February 18, 1778 he was commissioned a captain of engineers attached to Inspector General Steuben and then left the north to fight with Laurens. On October 9, 1779 he was wounded in his leg at Savannah while leading an advance guard. At the surrender of Charleston he was captured and was not exchanged until January 1782. He came to Philadelphia and by special resolution of Congress was made a major on May 2, 1783. The same year he was given a French pension of 300 livres and was made a captain of the French provincial forces.

In July and August he was with Steuben to secure the evacuation of the British from the northern border and in January 1784 he received honorable retirement from the American forces. At the request of Lafayette he made a portrait of Washington and designed the insignia and the diploma of the Society of the Cincinnati of which he was a member.

He returned to France but the next year returned to America. He enjoyed the friendship of Washington and both Hamilton and Morris had confidence in him. His pure and exalted ideals and integrity of character were recognized everywhere.

At Saint Paul's Church facing Broadway he designed the reredos and the communion rail. He was the designer of the Federal Hall, where Washington was inaugurated April 30, 1789 and for his work he was offered a payment of ten acres which he declined. Later he was offered 750 dollars which he declined as inadequate.

In Philadelphia he was the architect for a house built by Robert Morris and for a house built by John Nicholson, the partner of Morris.

He was appointed to design the plan of the new Federal City and enjoyed the confidence of Washington and Jefferson. In this design of the city that became the capital and was named for Washington he insisted that the hill where the Capitol stands and which is eighty-five feet above the river was the ideal site for the Capitol building. This was the spot that Daniel Carroll had intended for his manor house as it was the center of his country estate, Cerne Abbey. Carroll sold the property to the Government at so low a price that it was a gift to the United States.

PLATE XXXVI. City Hall, New York City as it looked in 1902. Major L'Enfant, Architect. (Photograph courtesy of the Museum of the City of New York.)

For his work upon the city plan L'Enfant was never paid as he should have been. He had found it impossible to continue working for the authorities and a fee of six hundred dollars was offered to him which he refused for ten years. Lots had been given to him near the White House but these were later sold for taxes.

During the War of 1812 he was employed upon Fort Washington on the Potomac and in the same year he was offered a professorship in civil and military engineering at West Point but this he declined. He enjoyed the friendship of the Carroll and Digges families and lived for awhile at the home of Thomas Digges near Fort Washington. Later he moved to Green Hill the estate of William Dudley Digges in Prince George County as Mrs. Digges was a daughter of Daniel Carroll, his friend. He died here and was buried on the farm in June of 1825.

In 1909 through the efforts of Bishop O'Connell of Richmond and Father Stafford of Saint Patrick's Church in Washington the body was brought to the Capitol and laid in state, the President being present and later he was buried in Arlington near where the tomb of the Unknown Soldier was later placed.

JOSEPH LEINFELDER was born in Itzing, Bavaria and was brought to this country when his parents settled in what is now called Avon, Ohio near Cleveland. Later his sister who had become a Franciscan in 1859 was elected as Superior General in 1863 and had him come to design a convent in Jefferson, Wisconsin where he also built for the sisters a large chapel. He designed in La Crosse, Wis. the Convent of Saint Rose.

LOUIS ADOLPHE LIVAUDAIS was born in New Orleans and spent his life there. He was a member of the firm of Favrot and Livaudais which did much work in the city. Among the buildings designed by the firm were the Saint Charles Theatre in 1901; the New Orleans Cotton Exchange in 1920; the Roosevelt Hotel in 1924; the Holton High School in 1926 and the Hutchinson Memorial Building at Tulane University. A member of the A.I.A. Died in 1932.

ANTHONY LOMBARDI was born in 1890 in Genaro, Foggia, Italy and was graduated from Columbia University in 1920. He was architect for the Board of Higher Education in New York and a member of the New York Society of Architects. Died Feb. 2, 1948.

THOMAS HALL LOCRAFT was born in Washington, D. C. Nov. 13, 1903. He was a student at The Catholic University of America where he received the degree of B. S. in architecture in 1927 and the degree of Ph.D. in 1931. He studied at the Fontainebleau School of Fine Arts in 1927 and won the Paris Prize in 1928. From that time until 1931 he studied at the Ecole in Paris. He received the Medal of the Societe des Architectes and a diploma of the French Government. He taught at the School of Architecture at Catholic University and later was its head. He was associated for many years with Frederick Vernon Murphy in the design of churches and other religious buildings. A president of the Washington, D. C. Chapter of the A.I.A.; vice-president of the Liturgical Arts Society; Society of Beaux Arts Architects. Died September 1, 1959.

CHARLES LUPPRIAN was born in 1878 and was known for his church work. Died Jan. 11, 1949.

PLATE XXXVII. Saint Stephen's Church, Geneva, New York. William V. Madden, Architect.

ELLIOTT LYNCH was trained in New York and in Paris. He was employed in the office of McKim Meade and White before establishing his own practice which was extensive in the early decades of the 20th century. Among his buildings are the churches of Saint Brendan, Saint Francis Xavier and Immaculate Heart of Mary all in Brooklyn; Church in Poughkeepsie the two latter in association with W. H. Orchard; a Baptist Church in Amherst, Mass. and a design submitted for the new Cathedral in Buffalo.

A member of The Architectural League from 1902 until 1928.

WILLIAM HENRY MACHEN who is thought of as one of the early painters of north west Ohio has been included in this survey of architects due to his work on the Lincoln Memorial in Springfield, Ill.

The Machen family had its origin in France where at the time of the Revolution Constant Jean Baptiste de Besse was a physician and vice mayor of Le Cateau in northern France. Ordered by leaders of the Revolution to arrest some Catholic priests and bring them to trial he allowed them to escape. For this act he was arrested and tried, sentenced to the guillotine two days after the murder of Louis 16th. He managed to escape by the aid of his brother and some gold. With his wife he wandered toward Germany and after a number of years settled in Holland. He had been forced to change his name and had taken that of his wife: Mecaine which was Germanized into Mechan. He lived in Holland until 1828. One of his sons married in Holland and he had a son baptized William Henry who was born February 10, 1832.

In 1847 when so many migrations to the United States were taking place the Mechan family came, motivated, largely by the fear that if they remained in Holland that the children would come under influences that would result in the loss of their Catholicity. The family settled first in Cleveland, Ohio but were influenced by Bishop Rappe to settle in Toledo which was a new settlement. Here William Machen grew to manhood and began the art work that engrossed him for life.

He contributed much to the religious culture of Toledo having served as organist in the Church of Saint Francis de Sales composing much of the music he played. He painted the Stations of The Cross which are still in place. Many portraits and landscapes were painted in Toledo. At the time of Lincoln's assassination his admirers determined upon a memorial in Springfield and held a competition for it. Thirty-one architects competed and Machen's design was among the finalists. For a period it was considered as the one to be used but the final selection was given to Larkin G. Mead, Jr. of Brattleboro, Vermont and Machen was given honorable mention.

Later he lived in Detroit where he taught art in Detroit College and at the Convent of The Sacred Heart in Grosse Pointe. When his son went to Washington he followed him and painted a number of notables there. He also was employed as an interpreter in the State Department as he had a knowledge of seven languages. This busy life ended June 19, 1911.

WILLIAM V. MADDEN was born in Rochester, N. Y. June 24, 1868. His family had been long settled in the city and he studied at the Mechanics' Institute. His architectural training was received in Rochester offices. Later with Edwin S. Gordon he opened offices and they had for many years an extensive practice. In Rochester the Church of Corpus Christi; the Church of Saint Peter and Paul; the Church of The Blessed Sacrament; the General Hospital and the Dental Dispensary.; Knights of Columbus Building; Sibley Building and the Church of Saint Stephen in Geneva, N. Y. Died Nov. 17, 1921.

PLATE XXXVIII. Chapel Trinity College, Washington, D. C. Maginnis and Walsh, Architects.

CHARLES DONAGH MAGINNIS was born in Londonderry, Ireland Jan. 7, 1867. He was educated at Cusack's Academy in Dublin and won honors in mathematics and drawing. He came to Boston early in life and was employed in the Office of Edmund M. Wheelwright, the city architect in 1885.

He established a reputation for his pen drawings and published a book: *Pen Drawing* that was highly regarded. In 1898 he with Timothy Walsh and Matthew Sullivan opened an office that received much work for many years. Later Mr. Sullivan withdrew and maintained his own office.

Among the buildings designed by Maginnis and Walsh were the new buildings for Boston College which were selected in a competition. Later buildings were those at Holy Cross College in Worcester, Mass.; the Law Building and some residence halls at Notre Dame; the Convent of the Carmelite Nuns in Santa Clara, Calif. which received the gold medal of the A.I.A. as did the design for the chapel at Trinity College in Washington, D. C.

Later the firm was appointed architects for the National Shrine of The Immaculate Conception in Washington and the Cathedral of Mary Our Queen in Baltimore.

The latter two buildings Mr. Maginnis was not destined to see built.

Many honors were conferred on him: the Laetare Medal given by Notre Dame; honorary degrees from Boston College, Holy Cross College, Tufts College and Harvard. He served two terms as President of the A.I.A. in 1937 and 1938. President of the International Congress of Architects held in Washington in 1938. In 1947 he received the gold medal of the A.I.A. for excellence in design; a member of the National Academy of Design; the National Institute of Arts of New York; Chairman of the State Art Commission; honorary corresponding member of the Royal Institute of British Architects.

Mrs. Maginnis was well known as the poet: Amy Brooks. He died Feb. 15, 1955 and his funeral Mass was largely attended by men prominent in state and professional life with a eulogy given by the Archbishop of Boston.

Charles Donagh Maginnis, Jr. was a graduate of Catholic University and was associated with his father until his death that preceded his father's by several years.

EDWARD F. MAHAR was born in Maryland in 1865 and studied at M.I.T. and in Paris. In 1907 he opened an office in Boston and designed many churches and rectories. One of these is the Church of Saint Francis of Assisi in Medford, Mass. He was described as the Dean of Boston draftsmen because of his skill and refinement of detail. Died May 10, 1937.

WILLIAM T. McCARTHY was born in 1877. He was graduated from Lehigh University. He was the architect of the Flatbush and Gowanus-Red Hook Housing project. Chairman of the Board of Brooklyn Charities. Died Apr. 20, 1952.

MAURICE J. McERLAIN was born Aug. 11, 1896 in South Bend, Ind. He was educated in local schools and studied at Notre Dame. He was associated for a number of years with Charles W. Cole and after retirement lived in Fort Myers, Fla. where he died in 1959.

HENRY McGILL of Brooklyn, N. Y. was born May 30, 1890. He studied in the Atelier of McLellan and Beadel. Later he was associated with Murphy and Dana and after Mr. Dana's death with Murphy and Hamlin. His work was premiated five times in the Parochial Buildings Award in the Borough of Queens.

PLATE XXXIX. Church of the Little Flower, Royal Oak. Michigan. Henry McGill, Architect. (Photography by The Detroit News.)

He designed the Church of The Little Flower in Royal Oak, Mich.; Saint Joseph College buildings in Brooklyn and churches in Detroit, Brooklyn and Astoria. Died in 1953.

JOSEPH H. McGUIRE was born in New York in 1865 and was graduated from City College and later studied at the College of Saint Francis Xavier. He had additional training at the Metropolitan Museum of Fine Arts and the Ecole des Beaux Arts in Paris.

He was architect for many churches in the vicinity of New York such as The Holy Family Church in New Rochelle, N. Y.; The Holy Trinity Church on 82nd Street; Saint Rose of Lima Church in Lima, N. Y.; Saint Elizabeth Hospital and church in New York and the Cathedral of The Sacred Heart in Richmond, Va. which had been provided for by Thomas Fortune Ryan and Mrs. Ryan.

During World War I he spent nine months in France as a secretary of the Knights of Columbus; a member of the A.I.A.; the Beaux Arts Society; the Catholic Club; Centre Club and Friendly Sons of Saint Patrick. He wrote: Before the Gay Nineties; Freezing with the Turks; Let's Go. Died Apr. 25, 1947.

WILBUR J. McELROY was born in London, England August 19, 1903, the son of an eminent American engineer who was a builder of railroads in many countries. The son was a graduate in architecture at Notre Dame in 1926. He worked in the office of Carrere and Hastings in New York and while there began the study of painting. Having ample means he designed such buildings as interested him; an enthusiastic sailor he designed and had built his own craft and he illustrated the book *Motor Boats* by William Atkin. His paintings are found in such collections as the Nelson Gallery in Kansas City, Mo. From his student years he was distinguished for his nobility of character which was the admiration of his associates. Died in Maine in 1942.

WILLIAM McGINTY was born in Saint Albans, Vermont and was educated in the Joyner Private School and then came to Boston where he practiced for several years and for a time with his brother John. He was the architect for Saint Ambrose Church and rectory in Dorchester, Mass.; the Richardson Building in Washington Street; the Butler Building in Canal Street and The Holy Ghost Hospital in Cambridge, Mass. He contributed to the Catholic World and wrote upon Catholic architecture, Irish art and architecture. Died Oct. 1, 1922.

JOSEPH McGINNIS, a native of Massachusetts, received the Rotch Scholarship in 1909 from Mass. Institute of Technology. After being established in practice he was architect of an addition to the Boston Public Library and Saint Paul's Church in Wellesley, Mass. He with his wife and child died during the great epidemic of 1918.

JOHN MAHONY of Philadelphia with Father Mallon worked upon the cathedral.

FRANK S. McMANUS of New York.

WALTER McQUADE was born in New York in 1889. He was a pupil of the Atelier Prevot. An architect for many years for the Port of New York Authority Bus Terminal. He acted as a consultant for the

PLATE XL. Cathedral of The Sacred Heart, Richmond, Virginia. Joseph McGuire, Architect. (Photograph courtesy of Richmond Chamber of Commerce.)

Johns Manville Corp. and for the Rising and Nelson Slate Company. During World War I he was in the Air Force. He was noted for his great skill in draughting and his detail plates, drawn with great skill, were features in architectural publications. For a number of years he was editor of *The Architect* a journal noted for its high quality which was published in New York City. Died Dec. 23, 1957.

JOSEPH FRANCOIS MANGIN was born and educated in France and came to this country as a refugee to join his brother in New York where they designed several buildings. He acted as an assistant to Vincent, the engineer-in-chief of the City's fortifications, and later succeeded him. He was made a Freeman of the City May 9, 1795 and a week later was appointed one of the city surveyors.

In partnership with Casimer T. Goerck he began in 1797 a city map published in 1803 which has been called "a magnificient example of drawing." Streets in the Corlears section were named for the two men. In 1797 he designed the New York State Prison. In 1802 he with John McComb, Jr. won a premium of 350 dollars for the design of a City Hall. Later the plans were revised for a smaller building. Critics consider that the design was by Mangin because of its French character of the period of Louis 16th and because McComb had never showed this character in his work. Probably McComb's only connection with the building was in the supervision of the construction. In 1798 the Mangin brothers designed the Park theatre and Brunel, their countryman, worked with them.

In 1802 the first Saint Patrick's Cathedral was started and its dedication took place on Ascension Day May 6, 1815. This was one of the first Gothic revival buildings to be built. This was the last recorded work of Mangin who left New York and no other details of his life have been found.

EMMITT G. MARTIN was born in La Salle, Ill. in 1889. He studied at the University of Illinois and went into the service in 1917. After this military experience he worked with his brother in Los Angeles. Later he was in independent practice and designed work in the vicinity of the city. Saint Brendan's Church in Los Angeles and Saint Augustine's Church in Culver City are examples of his work. Died Nov. 14, 1937.

EMANUEL LOUIS MASQUERAY was born in Dieppe, France on September 10, 1861. He was educated at Rouen and Paris. At the Ecole des Beaux Arts he won, in 1879, the Deschaumes Prize offered by the Institute of France; in 1880 the Chandesaigues Prize and a gold medal of the Paris Salon of 1883 were awarded to him.

In Paris he was an attache of the Commission des Monuments Historiques. At the Ecole he had known John M. Carrere, an American student, who advised him to come to America. This advice he followed and in 1887 he was with the young firm of Carrere and Hastings which had the patronage of Henry Folger, a railroad magnate of that period. Later he was with Richard Hunt. He founded the Atelier Masqueray as a place where young architects might be able to study design without going to Paris. It was the forerunner to the Beaux Arts Institute of Design. The latter had a great influence upon the architectural students in American schools during the first quarter of the 20th century.

In 1901 he was selected by the Commission of Architects of the Louisiana Purchase Exposition as the chief designing and consulting architect. He designed there the Cascades; the Colonnade of States and Pavilions; the Transportation, Agricultural, Horticultural, Fisheries and Forestry Buildings; the Louisiana Purchase Monument and twelve bridges.

PLATE XLI. Holy Ghost Hospital, Cambridge, Massachusetts. William McGinty, Architect.

While in Saint Louis he met Archbishop John Ireland of Saint Paul, Minn. who admiring his work, asked him to his See City and here he designed the Cathedral of Saint Paul; the Pro-Cathedral of Saint Mary in Minneapolis which is now a basilica; the Cathedral of Sioux Falls, S. D.; the Cathedral of The Immaculate Conception in Wichita, Kans.; the College of Saint James in Dubuque, Ia. and the new buildings at the College of Saint Thomas in Saint Paul. He was a great architect and was held in the highest respect by all and he won admiration for his tender care and devotion to his mother who had come to America and lived in Saint Paul. He was a member of the A.I.A. and the Architectural League of New York. Died May 26, 1917.

STUART MATHEWS whose nephews were the architects John and Robert Mitchell added a wing to the Saint Louis Hospital in 1832. The main portion was the work of Hugh O'Neil.

SAMUEL CHARLES GAETAN MAZZUCHELLI was born Nov. 4, 1806 in Milan, Italy one of the sixteen children of Luigi and Rachele Merlini, a family long prominent in the city as bankers. After the death of his mother he was sent to the Somaschi Fathers in Lugano, Switzerland. His father had hoped that the boy who was a co-lateral descendent of the Bramante family would take his place in the business life of Milan. Instead he showed so great a devotion to religion that at the age of seventeen he entered the Dominican novitiate in Faenza. In 1825 as a member of the Friars Preachers he went to Santa Sabina on the Aventine in Rome. He met Pope Gregory 16th and in 1827 he came to America.

As he had always an interest in architecture and was one of the few men who had any knowledge of it in the north west territory. He did much work and was recognized as an architect. Contracts regarding his employment for architectural services are still preserved in some of the county buildings. The town of Shullsburg, Wisconsin was laid out by him and the streets still bear the names given by Father Mazzuchelli such as Judgement Street which is the main street of the town and others such as Love, Goodness, Wisdom and Honor cross it. When he needed a church he designed it and among the many churches that are of his design are: Saint Anthony, Davenport, Ia.; the Cathedral of Saint Raphael in Davenport, Ia.; the Bishop's house; Saint Michael in Galena, Ill. Some of the churches have since disappeared but the church at New Diggins, Wis. called after Saint Augustine and built in 1844 in a Greco Gothic style is still standing. A tabernacle designed by him showing the same character as the "Little Temple" in Montorio done by his kinsman is in existence. He is considered to have designed the former state capitol in Iowa City although John F. Rague was its supervising architect; the Court House in Galena is another example of his secular designs. In spite of his activity as an architect and builder he was a great missionary priest throughout the territory. He was the founder of Sinsinawa Mound College and he founded the Dominican sisterhood in Sinsinawa, Wis. Died Feb. 23, 1864.

MAURICE P. MEADE was born in 1883 and was graduated from Mass. Institute of Technology in 1908. He practiced for years in Boston until his retirement in 1954. Among his designs is the Church of The Sacred Heart in North Quincy, Mass. Died Oct. 4, 1955.

P. E. MEAGHER of Saint Joseph, Mo. was architect of the Cathedral there and designed the Corby Memorial chapel near the city.

PLATE XLII. City Hall, New York City. McComb and Mangin, Architects. (Photograph courtesy of the Museum of the City of New York.)

ANTHONY F. MEROLLA was an architect in Lawrence and Boston. He was educated in the schools of Methuen, Mass. and was graduated from Washington Irving High School in New York in 1934. He was trained in the Architectural Center in Boston and after this period he worked in New York offices. He joined the army with which he served for four years in the Engineers Topographical Battalion with the rank of Technical Sergeant. This service was in this country, Algiers and Hawaii. After leaving the army he was chief draughtsman for Submarine Company until he joined the office of Sumner Schien in 1946 where he remained until his death. He was an organist and directed a number of musical plays; a member of The Holy Name Society; the K. of C.; the Massachusetts Association of Architects and the Boston Architects' Atelier and the Business and Professional Mens' Club in Lawrence. Died Aug. 13, 1954.

HENRY J. MEIER was born in Detroit in 1860 where he always lived. He joined John Donaldson in a firm that did many of the larger buildings in Detroit during their thirty-seven years association. A member of the Detroit Club; the Michigan Chapter of the A. I. A. and was offered appointment on the Detroit Building Commission. Died June 24, 1917.

WALTER R. MEIER was born in Detroit, July 8, 1887 the son of Henry J. Meier whose firm of Donaldson and Meier was well known in the city. He studied at Cornell in 1911 and after the death of his father became a member of the firm. During this time the David Stott Building in Detroit was built; a portion of the Penobscot Building; the Church of Saint Joseph in Port Huron; the Church of The Holy Redeemer in Detroit; the Church of Saint Vincent de Paul in Pontiac, Mich. and the Beaumont Tower in Lansing, Mich. A member of the A.I.A. Died March 12, 1931.

WILLIAM MINOGUE was born in 1903. He studied at Columbia and practiced in New York doing work for the Diocese. Among his buildings are La Salle Military Academy in Oakdale, L. I.; the building for Homeless Men at Greymoor, N. Y. and an office building in Sixth Avenue. He was a member of the K. of C. and the Friendly Sons of Saint Patrick. Died in 1955.

HENRY ANTHONY MINTON was born in Boston, Jan. 12, 1883. He was a graduate of Boston Latin School and received in 1903 the degree of A. B. cum laude from Harvard and in 1905 the degree of S. B. He later settled in California where his work was known from San Diego to Seattle. Died February 3, 1948.

JOHN F. MITCHELL was born in Ripley, Ohio in 1816 and came to Saint Louis in 1829. He became associated with his uncle, Stuart Mathews, who did much of the early building of Catholic churches and other structures in Saint Louis. Among Mitchell's churches are Saint Brigid's built in 1859; the Church of The Immaculate Conception in 1853. This was razed in 1874 when work on the tunnel endangered its walls. He also did Saint Joseph's Church in 1866.

ROBERT S. MITCHELL was a brother of John and was born in 1821. He was trained by his uncle, Stuart Mathews. He designed the Mercantile Library in 1854 and completed the Court House. He was lost at sea in 1883.

PLATE XLIII. Transportation Building, Louisiana Purchase Exposition, St. Louis, Missouri. E. L. Masqueray, Architect. (Photograph courtesy of the Missouri Historical Society.)

JOHN B. MOONEY was born in 1871 and lived for many years in New York. He designed three of the altars in the Church of Saint Paul the Apostle in New York which is an indication of his ability for this church is outstanding for the number of eminent artists whose work is seen in it. He was the architect for the present Herald and Post Building in Washington and the Hearst Building in New York. Died Dec. 2, 1956.

DENNIS XAVIER MURPHY was born in 1854 and was educated in Louisville, Ky., his native city. Many hospitals were designed by his firm such as Saint Agnes in Louisville; Saint Francis in Beach Grove; Saint Margaret in Hammond, Indiana; Saint Mary's in Emporia, Kansas; Saint Agnes Church in the same city and Saint Francis Hospital in Colorado Springs, Colo. Died Aug. 27, 1933.

JOHN CORNELIUS MURPHY, a brother of Dennis, was born in Louisville in 1864 and studied at the University of Louisville. Later he was associated with his brother. Died April 14, 1935.

PETER J. MURPHY, another brother, acted as resident architect and superintendent of the buildings designed by the firm. Born in 1868 he died July 11, 1955.

JAMES MURPHY was at the beginning of the 20th century an architect in San Antonio Texas and there did many buildings for Catholic parishes and for the Sisters of The Good Shepherd.

HENRY V. MURPHY was born in 1888 in Horseheads, N. Y. He was graduated from the Department of Architecture at Pratt Institute in Brooklyn and in this city he practiced his profession.

He was the architect for many buildings for both Catholic parish schools and for public schools. Some of his parish schools are the Archbishop Malloy High School in Jamaica; the Mary Louis Academy in Queen's; the Holy Family School and Convent at Hicksville, L. I.; Saint James School and Convent in Seaford, L. I.; For the New York City Housing Authority he designed the South Beach Houses in South Beach, S. I.; the Bushwick Health Center and the Domestic Relations Courthouse in the Civic Center Area in Brooklyn; many churches such as Our Lady of Refuge; Immaculate Heart of Mary; Saint Anselm's all in Brooklyn; Our Lady of Grace in Greensboro, N. C. and Saint Francis of Assisi in Norristown, Pa. He was architect for the general plan and the design of four of the buildings at Saint John's University in Brooklyn the total cost of the four being fourteen million dollars.

Many awards were made to him for his work including a gold medal for the altering of a block in Livingston Street; an award for the design of the Resurrection School in Rye, N. Y. in a national competition; from the Chamber of Commerce in Brooklyn for the design of Saint Peter Claver Community Center; a first award from the Chamber of Commerce of Queensboro for the Holy Child Church in Richmond Hill; the Liberal Arts Building at Saint John's University and the Archbishop Malloy High School both in Jamaica.

A member of the board of design for the Civic Center of Brooklyn and a member of the committee on religious buildings for the A.I.A. He was former president of the State Association of Architects and the Brooklyn Chapter of the A.I.A. A member of the Architectural League of N. Y., the Rotary Club and the Catholic Club of New York. Died May 18, 1960.

PLATE XLIV. First Capitol, Iowa City, Iowa. Rev. Samuel Muzzuchelli, Architect.

FREDERICK VERNON MURPHY was born in Fond du Lac, Wis. Feb. 16, 1879. He studied at George Washington University and at the Ecole des Beaux Arts in Paris where he received the Diploma of the French Government.

In 1910 he began at The Catholic University a course in architecture that produced students of outstanding ability and he continued this work for nearly forty years. During this time Murphy and Olmsted and later with Thomas Locraft he designed a number of important buildings such as the Mullen Library and the Martin Maloney Chemical Laboratory both at Catholic University; the Chapel at Saint Charles College in Catonsville, Md.; the Church of The Sacred Heart at Chevy Chase, Md.; the Church of Saint Francis de Sales in Buffalo, N. Y.; and Saint Mary's Church in Mobile, Ala. A Fellow of the A.I.A.; Chevalier of the Legion of Honor; the gold medal for the design of the Sacred Heart Church and the Mullen Library; member of the International Society of Architects; member of the Cosmos and University Clubs of Washington. Died April, 1958.

FATHER JOSE ANTONIO DE JESUS MARIA DE MURGUIA was born Dec. 10, 1715 at Domayguia Alva, Spain and came to Mexico as a layman. He became a Franciscan Jan. 29, 1736 and was ordained in 1744. He served as a missionary in Sierra Gorda until 1748 for nineteen years and built the first masonry church of San Miguel. He was sent to California in 1768 and founded the Mission of Santa Clara where he was architect, director and laborer. Died May 12, 1783.

JAMES W. NAUGHTON was born in Ireland in 1840 and came to Brooklyn with his parents at an early age. In 1874 he was superintendent of buildings in Brooklyn and in 1875 City Superintendent of Public Schools and architect for Erasmus School. Died Feb. 26, 1898.

JOHN P. NIERNSEE was born in Vienna in 1823. He was educated at the University of Prague and studied with Schinkel in Berlin and with Kramer in Prague. He acted as a surveyor and draftsman in the army engineering offices before coming to this country. He was employed by Benjamin Latrobe and in the engineering department of the Baltimore and Ohio Railroad. With a partner, J. Crawford Neilson, he designed the chapel at Greenmount Cemetery and in 1850 Grace Protestant Episcopal and Emmanuel churches all in Baltimore.

In June 1856 he went to Columbia, S. C. to be the architect of the new state capitol. This work had to be suspended in 1861 at the outbreak of the war. He served with the Confederate Army and received the rank of major. Due to the fire started by the invading Northern army about seven hundred thousand dollars worth of work on the buildings was destroyed and the architect's drawings. As the state was unable to continue building the architect returned to Baltimore in 1865. He resumed practice there and designed the Carrolton Hotel; the Academy of Music; the Y.M.C.A.; the orphanage; the Hopkins Buildings on Second Street and the Chamber of Commerce Building.

He was called back to Columbia to resume work on the Capitol in 1885 but died in June of that year. A later architect changed the design of the central feature much to the regret of the people of the state. This architect was dismissed and Frank Niernsee, the son of the original architect was secured to continue the work on the building. However, the central feature was not changed to the original design of his father. Frank Niernsee had done other work such as the Opera House in Lynchburg, Va. and work at Chester, S. C.

PLATE XLV. Sacred Heart Seminary, Detroit, Michigan. Donaldson and Meier, Architects. (Photograph by The Detroit News.)

ARTHUR L. O'BRIEN was born in San Francisco in 1876 and was trained in local offices. He was associated with his brother upon commercial work. Died July 29, 1924.

MATTHEW O'BRIEN was born in 1871 in San Francisco and died April 25, 1920.

JAMES L. O'CONNOR was born in New Orleans in 1870 and was educated there and in Galveston, Tex. He received his architectural training in Austin and was the architect for the Main Building of the University of Texas and the State School for the Deaf in Abilene. Died in 1902.

L. J. O'CONNOR practiced in New York where he was the architect of Saint Agnes Church on 43rd Street built in 1876 and Saint Mary's church, now the Cathedral in Syracuse, N. Y.

MICHAEL J. O'CONNOR was born in San Francisco in 1860. He was educated there and at the School of Mines at Columbia University, where he was graduated in 1881. He was employed for several years as a draughtsman in New York and later became a member of the firm of Little and O'Connor. He was the architect for the College of Pharmacy; the Flagler house on Park Avenue and the country houses of the Gilbert and Brokaw families at Great Neck, L. I. Died July 24, 1936.

P. J. O'CONNOR was born in Liverpool, England and was educated in Ireland and in Rome. He returned to Dublin and studied architecture there before he came to the United States. For a period he was in Philadelphia and on June 18, 1852 he went to California where he spent the remainder of his life in San Francisco.

THOMAS O'GRADY in practice in Boston in 1888.

PATRICK M. O'MEARA was born in 1890 in West Bend, Wis. where he received his early education before he came to Notre Dame. He worked in various offices and then formed the partnership of Damon and O'Meara which lasted for six years. Later he was with James B. Hills and then alone until the formation of the firm that included Messrs. Maguolo and Quick. Much work came to the firm throughout the Mississippi Valley. The De Paul Hospital in Saint Louis was awarded the Certificate of Merit in 1930 by the Chamber of Commerce. Numerous churches and college buildings as well as many hospitals have come to the firm. A member of the A.I.A. Died Oct. 24, 1948.

JEREMIAH O'ROURKE was born in Dublin, Ireland Feb. 6, 1833. He was educated at the Dublin School of Design and came to the United States in 1850. He worked in the office of the Supervising Architect and designed postoffices in Buffalo and Kansas City.

With his sons opened offices in Newark, N. J. and among the buildings of the firm were the Church of The Immaculate Conception in Camden, N. J.; Saint John's in Orange, N. J.; Holy Cross in Harrison, N. J.; Saint Michael's Hospital in Newark and the Dominican Convent there. He started the Cathedral of The Sacred Heart in Newark but his work was taken over by another firm shortly after the initiation of the work. A member of the A.I.A. Died April 22, 1915.

BERNARD O'ROURKE was born in 1857 and died in 1919.

PLATE XLVI. Capitol Building, Columbia, South Carolina. John Niernsee, Architect. (Reproduced from the Collections of the Library of Congress.)

WILLIAM P. O'ROURKE died in 1921.

ALLISON OWENS was born in New Orleans on Dec. 29, 1869 a son of General William M. and Caroline Zachariel Owens. He was graduated from Tulane University in 1888 and studied at Mass. Institute of Technology from 1892 until 1894. He was the architect of the Criminal Court Building; the Public Library and Notre Dame Seminary; Sacred Heart Convent; work for the Sisters of The Blessed Sacrament.

In the Mexican border campaign in 1916 he served with the rank of major; as colonel in the 141 F. A. in 1918 and in 1919 in France; a brigadier general in 1924. He was made a Chevalier of the Legion of Honor and was a member of the Knights of Columbus; Saint Vincent de Paul Society; President of the Associated Catholic Charities. Died Jan. 30, 1951.

GABRIEL PAUL was born in Santo Domingo to a family of wealth and distinction. In 1781 he and his elder brother were sent to college in France. In 1802 he came with his mother to Baltimore and in 1806 to Saint Louis. Here he was married to Miss Louise Choteau, the daughter of Colonel Auguste Choteau who was considered the first citizen of the city.

In 1818 Paul was appointed as architect for the Cathedral, the only church of any architectural pretensions in that great area. It was a brick structure on the same plot of ground now occupied by the Church of Saint Louis of France at Second and Walnut Streets. He also designed the Berthold mansion in 1821, a brick building designed after the type of house found in Maryland. This was probably due to his having lived there as had Bartholomew Berthold, the owner. Another example of his work is the Carr house. He died in 1845 and was buried in Calvary Cemetery where the grave is marked by an interesting old monument.

GABRIEL PAQUE worked in New Orleans in 1806.

FATHER PATERNA was one of the builders of the Mission of San Gabriel in California.

FERNAND PARMENTIER was born in Paris in 1865 the son of an army officer. He was educated there and then came to Chicago where he was employed and in 1893 went to Santa Barbara and then to Los Angeles. He was the architect for the French Hospital and for apartment houses and residences. He entered the army in 1914 and fought in Alsace. Later he was transferred to the Dardenelles where he was killed at Seddal Behr in 1915. A Fellow of the A.I.A.

FATHER FRANCISCO PALOU was born at Palma Mallorca in 1722. He worked in California where he died at San Francisco in 1790.

MOTHER JOSEPH PARIZEAU of the Sisters of Charity of Providence was born in Montreal in 1820 and when twenty-one she became a member of the community in Montreal. She had worked with her father who was a joiner and builder and thus received a certain training in architecture that was to be of good help when she was confronted with pioneering work in the United States. With five other sisters she went by way of the Isthmus of Panama and arrived in Fort Vancouver, Washington, Dec. 8, 1856. Here

PLATE XLVII. DePaul Hospital, Saint Louis, Missouri. Patrick M. O'Meara, Architect. (Photograph by Piaget Studio.)

they founded the first permanent school and hospital in the Northwest section of the country. For forty years she was engaged in building institutions for the young, aged and needy, designing the buildings, supervising the construction and in many cases working on the decorations of the interiors. Her drawing instruments are still preserved in Providence Academy in Vancouver which was one of the buildings she worked on. Others are Saint Joseph's Hospital in Seattle; Sacred Heart Hospital in Spokane; Saint Elizabeth's in Yakima and Saint Joseph's Hospital in Vancouver. Examples of her wood carving on altars, embroidery of vestments and other examples of her work she found time to do in addition to building, are still preserved.

From the small beginnings there are now seventy institutions found on the Pacific coast from Washington to Alaska. When the A.I.A. met in Seattle it was declared that Mother Joseph had performed all the functions of an architect. She died in 1902.

ANDREW G. PATRICK was born in Bridgeport, Conn. on Nov. 28, 1907. He lived later in Stratford and attended the University School there, He was graduated from Notre Dame in 1931. For a period he worked with the U. S. Coast and Geodetic Service and for the U. S. Army at Fort Wright and later with an architectural firm in Bridgeport. While there he was the designer of the present parish school of Saint James and he remodelled the church.

In his own office he designed the Church of Our Lady of Good Counsel in Bridgeport; Saint Stephens Church in Stepney, Conn.; the Second Hill Lane elementary school; Birdseye School; Our Lady of Grace Church; the rectory, school and convent of the Church of The Holy Name of Jesus; Our Lady of Peace Church and parish hall; the residence of the Bishop. He was a member of the A.I.A. and a charter member of the Connecticut Society of Architects; the Stratford Historical Society; Knights of Columbus. Died May 2, 1954.

EMILIE PERROT was born in Philadelphia Nov. 12, 1872. He was graduated from the University of Pennsylvania in 1896. Later he was a member of the firm of Ballinger and Perrot which was well known for its work in re-inforced concrete construction. He developed the unit girder frame system of construction that was officially adopted by the U. S. Government. He lectured at the University of Pennsylvania for many years upon concrete construction. He was the author of many papers and articles upon the subject. The firm designed among many buildings: Villa Maria College at Immaculata, Pa.; Chapel of Saint Joseph's Novitiate at Metuchen, N. J.; the library at Fordham University; Good Counsel College at White Plains, N. Y.; industrial buildings for the American Viscose Plant at Marcus Hook; original buildings for Victor Talking Machine Co. in Camden, N. J.; the industrial village of Marcus Hook; Park Gardens at Wilmington, Del.

In the First World War he was architect for the Government Emergency Ship Building Corp. He was a member of The Men of Malvern; Catholic Alumni Society of Philadelphia; Am. Society of Civil Engineers; Engineers' Club of Philadelphia; Fourth Degree of the K. of C. and an L.L.D. of Saint Joseph's College. Author of *Ground Work of Architecture*. Died Feb. 7, 1954.

FATHER ANTONIO PEYRI was born at Parera, Catalonia, Jan. 10, 1755. He worked at San Luis Rey in 1802. Died in 1934.

PLATE XLVIII. Old Cathedral, St. Louis, Missouri. Cabriel Paul, Architect. (Photograph by E. Boehl. Courtesy of the Missouri Historical Society.)

WENDELL T. PHILLIPS was born in Milford, Mass. Aug. 5, 1887 the son of William and Ellen Kelliher Phillips who were natives of Ireland. He received his architectural degree at Notre Dame in 1912. He went to the office of Maginnis and Walsh where he worked from 1912 until 1940. He then opened an office in Milford and for a number of years was architect for the Diocese of Springfield, Mass. He designed many churches, among them The Immaculate Conception Church in Lancaster, Mass.; Saint Patrick's in Chicopee Falls; Saint Jaques in Taunton; Saint Roch in Oxford all being in Massachusetts.

In Thompsonville, Conn. he did Saint Patrick's Church. His last work was Saint Theresa's Church in Pittsfield, Mass. Among the schools was Notre Dame Academy in Worcester.

He received the honorary degree of M. A. from Holy Cross College in 1925. He was a member and Chairman of the Mass. Board of Registration for Architects from 1950 to 1955. Member of the A.I.A. Died Feb. 27, 1955.

ANTON POHL was working in Charleston, S. C. in the early part of the 19th century where he designed the church of The Holy Cross.

PIERRE PORTOIS was born in Gau, Belgium in 1812. He came to America and to San Francisco in 1851 as one of the very early settlers of the city. He did many of the older buildings among which were the Hibernian Bank, the Commercial Hotel. During his later years he became greatly interested in the study of political economy and had a wide correspondence with statesmen and writers upon the subject. He died August 20th, 1900 and his funeral was from the French church of Notre Dame des Victoires.

THOMAS H. POOLE was born in 1860 and worked in New York principally for Catholic clients. Among the buildings from his office were the Cardinal Gibbons Memorial in Washington, D. C.; Holy Cross Academy in the same city; Saint Francis Xavier College on 16th Street in New York. Died July 31, 1919.

GEORGE H. PROVOT was born in New York City in 1869. He spent nine years at school in France where he received a B. S. degree and then returned to America. In 1886 he entered Columbia and three years later he received the Ph. D. degree in architecture. As a member of the firm of Welch, Smith and Provot much work was done. Later he practiced alone and designed the old French Hospital on W. 34th Street; alterations made to the Brevoort Hotel. He was active in Franco-American interests and was associated with several realty companies as secretary and director. Died July 10, 1936.

WILFRID E. PROVOT was born in 1884 and was the architect for the Diocese of Manchester, N. H. He designed The Sacred Heart Hospital; Saint Joseph's Hospital; Our Lady of Perpetual Help Church; the West Manchester High School; Saint Joseph's School, Keene, N. H. and the Convent of The Precious Blood, Brooklyn, N. Y. Died Oct. 7, 1941.

JACQUES NICHOLAS BUSSIERE de POUILLY was born in 1805 at Chatel Censoir, Burgogne, France. He was educated at Rouen and at the Ecole des Beaux Arts in Paris. With his brother Isadore who was trained as an architect they settled in New Orleans about 1830 and are regarded as the earliest architects of note in that city due to their training and to the ability shown in their work. In 1835 they

PLATE XLIX. St. Paul's Cathedral, Pittsburgh, Pennsylvania. Egan and Prindiville, Architects. (Reproduced from the Collections of the Library of Congress.)

111

were the architects for the Saint Louis Hotel which was considered an outstanding and remarkable building. A notable feature of the design was the dome over a circular plan and the constructional solution of it. The cost of the hotel when it was built was over a million and a half dollars. Eight designs had been submitted for it and the design of the de Pouilly brothers was the one selected.

CHARLES H. PRINDEVILLE was born in 1868, his family having come to Chicago in 1838. He worked in Chicago offices and then entered a partnership with James J. Egan and this lasted for a number of years. The firm did many ecclesiastical structures including Saint Xavier's College in Chicago and Mercy Hospital. In Pittsburgh was built the Cathedral of Saint Paul.

At one time President of the Illinois Chapter of the A.I.A. and a member of the Illinois Society of Architects. Died June 17, 1947.

JACQUES RAMEE is among the few architects in America who have had the varied commissions and unusual clients that relied upon Ramee to solve their problems.

Ramee was born in Charlemont, Ardennes, France on April 18, 1764. At first he was destined to study for the priesthood but he seemed to show such interest in building that his uncle, a canon in the Cathedral of Louvain, who had the supervision of his studies provided him with opportunities to study architecture. It is said that as early as twelve years he was helping army engineers to plan their fortifications. At sixteen he was in Paris and after a few months he was appointed to the building staff of the Comte d'Artois, a younger brother of the King.

In 1786 he had designed a house with a circular roof; then he was employed by William Beckford to design a magnificent tent in the Oriental fashion to be erected in Paris where Beckford wished to entertain. Later this was moved to the shores of Lake Geneva for Beckford's elaborate parties. Ramee was called there to direct these entertainments.

As the Revolution drew near in France he joined the Revolutionary army and rose to the rank of Captain. When he denounced the insults offered to the King he became a suspect and found it necessary to leave the country.

He passed through many of the small states that composed Germany. At Erfurt he worked for the prince primate, then for the princes of Saxe-Meinungen, Gotha and Weimer. In 1803 he designed in Hamburg the Borsenhalle which the German architect Weinbrenner declared "was the most beautiful and most skillfully designed in Europe at the time." Another design was for a theatre for the French refugees and he did many park and garden designs.

The King of Denmark and the Prince of Mecklinburg-Schwerin were glad to have him work for them as were many of their subjects. In Hamburg the great merchant, John Parish, thought highly of him and employed him for his buildings. When Parish was forced to leave the city and his beautiful estate due to the French invasion Ramee thought of returning to Paris. He was spared this and instead listened to the proposals of David Parish to come to America.

David Parish had acquired immense tracts of land in northern New York and wished to develop the property. He bought from the Ogden family the site of the present city of Ogdensburgh and established Parishville. He needed Ramee who fitted so well his requirements and as a consequence many houses and estates were built at this time from the designs of the architect.

On one occasion when returning to Philadelphia, Parish brought the architect with him and they

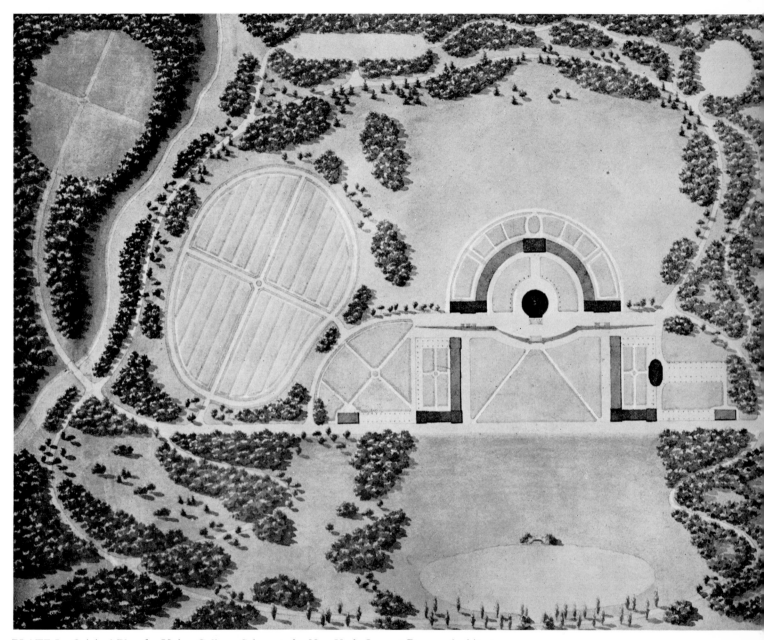

PLATE L. Original Plan for Union College, Schenectady, New York. Jacques Ramee, Architect.

stopped in Schenectady. There Ramee found a new opportunity; the lay-out of Union College and the design of its buildings. His design showed the first unified group of college buildings in the United States. This design in 1813 preceded the design of Jefferson's for the University of Virginia. The flanking buildings were built but the central building was not carried out until many years later and then by another architect and in another style.

Back in Baltimore Ramee was employed by David Smith to design a great estate and with this client's backing Ramee tried to secure the work on the Baltimore Exchange. This he failed to obtain and in 1816 he returned to Europe where he settled in Paris in 1821. On May 18, 1842 he died at Bourains near Noyon.

DANIEL RAMEE who had been born in Hamburg on May 16, 1816 came to America with his Father and later returned with him to Europe. There he became known for his medieval studies and was appointed to restore the Cathedrals of Noyon, Senlis and Beauvais and the Abbeys of Saint Riquier and Saint Wulfranc at Abbeville.

He travelled much in England, Italy and Germany and produced a great number of books upon architecture and its history. Some of these he translated into English and Dutch and many have been translated by others. He died in 1887.

JAMES A. RANDALL was born in Syracuse, N. Y. Dec. 21, 1861, the son of Colonel James Randall who was a prominent builder in Syracuse. After his training at the local schools he entered the office of James H. Kirby. Later he was a partner of Mr. Kirby. Then he became associated with another architect and later with his nephew. He and his associates were the architects for The Syracuse Public Library; the Church of The Sacred Heart; the Blodgett Vocational High School; the rectory of the Cathedral and many public schools. In Solvay they designed the Carnegie Library and in Oswego the high school.

He was prominent in tennis and golf in Syracuse; a member of the Board of Managers of the Newark State School; a President of the Citizens' Club; a founder of the Sedgewick Farm Club; Chamber of Commerce; Onondaga Historical Association; Century Club; K. of C. and had held office in the A.I.A. Died June 12, 1940.

BURGESS J. REEVES was born in London Feb. 15, 1846. He practiced a number of years there before coming to Los Angeles in 1881. He was the architect at the old Cathedral and at Saint Vincent's Church. Died in April, 1936.

ALBAN H. REEVES the son of Burgess was born in London in 1869 and was educated there and trained in the office of his father before coming to this country. He worked for several years in New York and then went to Los Angeles where he was in practice until his death May 17, 1916.

OLIVER REAGAN was born in Terre Haute, Ind. on Mar. 14, 1891. He received the degree of B. S. in Architecture in 1912 from Rose Polytechnic Institute in that city. He later studied at Columbia and had an A.E.F. Art Scholarship in 1919 for study in France. In 1921 he received the Le Brun Travelling Scholarship.

In New York he became a member of the firm of Voorhees, Walker and Smith. This firm was known for its many notable buildings such as the New York Federal Reserve Bank; the Department of Com-

PLATE LI. University Club, Chicago, Illinois. Holabird and Roche, Architects. (Photograph by Architectural Record Co. (Reproduced from the Collections of the Library of Congress.)

merce Building in Washington and the Temple of Religion at the New York World's Fair. He was a consultant for the new work at the Beekman Downtown Hospital in New York and the general plan of Fairfield University. He was architect for many churches in Connecticut: Saint Joseph's in Canaan; Saint Anthony in Litchfield; the Immaculate Heart of Mary in Harwinton; Our Lady of Grace in Stamford. For the Church of The Assumption in Westport he designed an altar and the parish school. During the World War I he was a First Lieutenant in the Air Service Construction Division from 1917 until 1919 in the A.E.F. A member of the A.I.A.; a founder and Director of the Liturgical Arts Society; member of Alpha Tau Omega.

Author of Architecture of Tuscany; American Architecture of the Twentieth Century. Died June 2, 1958.

PERSEO RIGHETTI practiced in San Francisco, Cal.

MARTIN ROCHE was born in Cleveland on August 15, 1855 and was brought to Chicago by his parents in 1857. He received his early education there and at seventeen entered the employ of William Le Baron Jenney. No better place could be found to acquire a sound preparation for his profession. Later he began a practice with William Holabird and this continued until the death of Mr. Holabird. The firm did an immense amount of important work. Among the earlier buildings were the Cook County Court House; the La Salle and Sherman Hotels; the University Club; Vendome Building; Monroe Building; John Crerar Library; Rosenwald Hall at the University of Chicago.

Later work during the remaining years of Mr. Roche's life after the death of his partner in 1923 were the Palmer House; the Stevens Hotel, one of the largest in the world; the Daily News Building and the Board of Trade Building. Outside of Chicago were designed such buildings as the Schroeder Hotel in Milwaukee; the Muhlbach Hotel in Kansas City, Mo.; the Nicollet Hotel in Minneapolis and the Chicago Stadium.

He was a member of the Western Association of Architects; Fellow of the A.I.A.; a director of the Chicago Art Institute; a director of the University and a member of the Board of Advisors of Illinois. Died June 6, 1927.

WILLIAM RODRIGUEZ was a descendent of refugees from Santo Domingo and received his training in this country. He was a brother-in-law of the famous Archbishop John Hughes of New York. In 1832 he designed the Church of Saint John the Evangelist in Philadelphia for the future Archbishop who was then its pastor. After this in New York he was architect for the Church of The Transfiguration of Our Lord built on Mott Street. This church had been founded by Father Varela, a noted priest of that period in the city. He was architect for the Church of Saint Francis in 1852 which was designed in classic style. Associated later with James Renwick on the design of the new Saint Patrick's Cathedral on Fifth Avenue. It is interesting to notice that one never hears of his connection with this important church which according to the perspective published in 1850 shows the design of a robust character and this drawing has the names of the architects as Renwick and Rodriguez. According to a contract of March 5th, 1859 each architect was to receive a payment of 2500 dollars for eight years. It is interesting to note the design of Grace church which had been built at an earlier period by Renwick and which shows few of the characteristics of Saint Patrick's. Was this later character the contribution of Rodriguez? Shortly after the start of the building his health failed.

PLATE LII. Cathedral of New York City. Renwick and Rodriguez, Architects. (Reproduced from the Collections of the Library of Congress.)

117

HUGH D. ROQUET was an architect brought from France by Bishop de la Hailandiere and he did some work at the Cathedral of Vincennes, Ind. and the old Academy of Saint Mary of the Woods near Terre Haute. Later he built the village church and the Vandenburgh County Court House. He lived near the village of Saint Mary of the Woods where he died in 1856.

JOHN ROGERS was born in Ireland in 1785 of a Catholic mother who had him baptized but after her death he was reared a Presbyterian by his uncle, Sir Arthur Rogers. When he came to America in 1804 he settled in Baltimore and there he noticed an old negro, a slave, reading daily a Catholic prayer book. Through this example he returned to the religion of his mother.

   He was commissioned by Bishop Flaget to build his Cathedral in Bardstown, Ky. and this was the first Cathedral west of the Alleghenies. Its corner stone was laid on July 16, 1816. Rogers in addition to his profession was known as a wood carver and musician. The remainder of his life was spent about Louisville where his descendents still live.

FATHER JOSE BERNARDO SANCHEZ was born in 1776 at Robledillo, Spain and became a Franciscan Oct. 9, 1794. In February 1803 he left Spain for the college in Mexico. In August 1804 he was in California and from 1804 until 1820 he was in San Diego. Then a year was spent at Purissima as President when he was sent to San Gabriel where he remained until his death Jan. 16, 1833.

DANIEL SANTORO an architect who practiced many years on Staten Island was born in 1880. He founded the Italian Mens' Club and was prominent in political affairs. Founded the Staten Island Italian Historical Society. Died Dec. 1, 1954.

GEORGE J. SCHELL was chief architect for D. H. Burnham and Co. for many years from 1891. He designed buildings at the World's Fair in Chicago in 1893 and for the Fair of 1933; the Burnham Building; Carbon and Carbide Building, Bankers' Building and the Engineering Building. Died 1955.

J. W. SCHICKEL was born in Wiesbaden in 1850 where he was a pupil of William Bozler. He travelled in France, Italy and Germany and came to the United States in 1870. He did much work such as the churches of: Holy Trinity; Saint Leonard; All Saints and Saint Nicholas in Brooklyn; the Abbey church in Latrobe; Saint Louis church in Buffalo; Saint Joseph's Seminary in Yonkers, N. Y.; the exterior of the Cathedral of The Sacred Heart in Newark, N. J.; Saint Ignatius church in New York City and the Lenox and Saint Vincent's Hospitals in the same city. Died June 1, 1907.

HENRY J. SCHLACKS was born in Chicago in 1868. He was educated there and for awhile was in the office of Adler and Sullivan. He then studied at Mass. Institute of Technology and extensively in Europe. He designed many railroad stations for western railroads such as the Big Four Station at Greencastle, Ind.; the Denver and Rio Grande Station at Salt Lake City and for the same railroad the station and offices at Grand Junction, Colo. Many parish buildings were his work: Saint Francis Xavier Church in Wilmette, Ill.; Saint Joseph's Church in La Salle, Ill.; buildings at Mt. St. Joseph's College at Dubuque, Ia. In Chicago he did Saint Paul's Church which is one of the earlier uses of Guastavino construction as it is masonry throughout; Saint Ita's Church and Saint Mary's of the Lake; Saint Martin's

PLATE LIII. Cathedral, Bardstown, Kentucky. John Rogers, Architect. (Reproduced from the Collections of the Library of Congress.)

119

and Saint Anthony's Hospital. In 1898 he was in charge of the first architectural courses at Notre Dame leading to a degree. A member of the A.I.A. Died Jan. 6, 1938.

VICTOR SCHULTZ was born in Germany but at an early age was brought to Pennsylvania where he learned the carpenter trade. He came to Wisconsin in 1840 at first to Janesville and then to Milwaukee. He built the first swing bridge over the Milwaukee River and became known as an architect and builder. He was greatly interested in church architecture and was given the commission to design Saint Mary's Church in the city. Later he was appointed architect of the new Cathedral of Saint John that was to be built in Milwaukee. He was architect of Trinity Church but in 1854 it was decided to build a seminary at Saint Francis. This work was in the country and occupied him the rest of his professional life as he settled in the vicinity of the seminary and remained there until his death in 1890. The Wisconsin Magazine of History states: "Without a doubt, the best piece of work of any of the old time architects as far as design is concerned is Saint John's Cathedral. Mr. Schultz was undoubtedly a man of culture, as the entire design of the lower portion of the Cathedral shows the hand of a master designer. The work has all the characteristic marks of the late German Renaissance style of architecture and no doubt reflects Schultz' early environment and training."

JOSEPH SCHWARZ was born in New York City, Feb. 24, 1856. His parents moved to La Crosse, Wis. and he received his architectural training there and in 1884 he opened an office in Sioux Falls, S. D. where he practiced the remainder of his life. He was an organist of ability and served in the churches of the city. Died Dec. 26, 1927.

JOHN F. SHEBLESSEY was born in Chicago July 4, 1873. He studied at a commercial school and while working as a stenographer studied at the Art Institute and was graduated from Armour Institute of Technology. He worked in the Office of Henry Ives Cobb and Holabird and Root in Chicago. Later he practiced alone in Cincinnati. He designed many schools and churches in Ohio and Kentucky. Among these are the church of The Holy Trinity and Saint Bonaventura Monastery. In Kentucky he designed Nazareth College buildings. A member of the A.I.A. Died 1939.

EDWARD A. SCHILLING was born in Auburn, N. Y. Nov. 7, 1871 where he was first educated. In 1887 he came to Detroit and studied architecture and received his first office training. Later he travelled for study in Europe.

He was in the firm of Van Leyen, Schilling and Keough which lasted until 1933. After this he practiced alone. He was architect for the American Legion Building in Detroit; Belle Isle Casino; Fordson High School; churches of Saint Theresa, Saint Agnes, Saint Thomas and Saint Rose; Saint Peter's Cathedral in Marquette, Mich. and the Newberry State Hospital.

He was one of the founders of the Detroit Architectural Sketch Club and its first secretary. In 1915 he became the first secretary of the Board of Registration of Architects. He was one of the early promoters of city planning for Detroit. When the City Plan Commission was formed in 1919 he became a member and later its president and served until 1940. He was appointed a member of the Zoning Board of Appeals and was its president at the time of his death. For two years he was president of the Michigan Society of Architects. A member of the A.I.A. Died Sept. 11, 1952.

PLATE LIV. Denver and Rio Grande Railroad Station, Salt Lake City, Utah. Henry J. Schlacks, Architect. (Photograph by Wood Studios.)

RICHARD J. SHAW was born in Boston and studied in the Harvard Graduate School of Design where he was graduated in 1912. He was employed in local offices and in 1917 was a superintendent of construction in Newport, R. I. Later he was associated with Timothy G. O'Connell and the firm did a great deal of work throughout New England in the designing of churches and other ecclesiastical buildings. Later he was alone and was the architect of Brighton School; Corpus Christi Church in Auburndale and the much admired Convent of The Immaculate Conception in Malden, Mass.; Boston Fire Alarm Headquarters. He was the winner four times of the Harleston Parker Medal for outstanding work; a member of the Massachusetts Society of Architects; Massachusetts Art Commission; State Examination Board of Registration; member of the Harvard Club of Boston. Died August 24, 1958.

WILLIAM D. SHEA was associated with his brother Frank and their work was largely about San Francisco. They were the architects of the churches of Saint Vincent de Paul; Holy Cross; Star of the Sea. After the earthquake of 1906 they were in charge of repairs to the dome of the City Hall and architects of the Elks Club of Santa Rosa. A member of the A.I.A. Frank Shea died in 1929 and his brother William July 17, 1931.

JOHN SLOAN was born in New York and studied architecture at New York University. He practiced in New York and from 1908 until 1911 he was in the Philippines. At Front Royal, Va. he supervised the Army's Remount Depot. In 1915 he was a captain in the Aviation Section of the Signal Corps in charge of construction work at Langely Field near Hampton, Va. In World War I he had been in construction work for the American Expeditonary Force; from 1919 to 1920 he was a member of the Army Air Service Advisory Board in Washington.

In 1920 he became architect for the Pershing Square Building. Due to his interest in racing he was appointed by the Governor of New York to give firm control over horse racing in that state. From 1934 until 1942 he was a member of the State Racing Commission and did much to correct abuses.

For over thirty years he was in practice in New York City in the firm of Sloan and Robertson and later as Sloan Associates. He designed many tall buildings and supervised construction as an engineer and was active in the promotion of many of these buildings. He defended such tall buildings against European critics. Some of the work of his firms were the Irving House Cardiac Home for Children; a twenty story addition to the Saint Regis Hotel at 35th and Fifth Avenue; Hippodrome de Las Americas in Mexico City and similar buildings in other racing centers; the Chanin Building of fifty-six stories; the Graybar Building of thirty-two stories; the Maritime Exchange of thirty-five stories; Ward's Island Disposal Plant costing thirty million dollars and the West Side Highway architectural features costing sixteen millions. Other buildings were the New York State Exhibit Amphitheatre and stage for the New York World's Fair; many hospitals and state institutions such as the Nurses' Home at Harlem Hospital and other buildings there; the Ricker's Island Penitentiary; the State Teachers' College at Indiana, Pa. and the House of Detention in New York City. Died June 24, 1954.

JOHN L. SMITHMEYER was born in Austria in 1832. His family was a notable one but as a boy of sixteen he became involved in the revolution of 1848 and had to leave the country. He settled in Chicago, moved then to Terre Haute and later to Indianapolis. During the Civil War he was in charge of an Indiana district artillery depot. Later he was in the office of the Supervising Architect and worked in the South.

PLATE LV. Graybar
Building, New York City.
John Sloan, Architect.
(Photograph by Irving Un-
derhill. Reproduced from
the Collections of the Library of Congress.)

123

In 1872 he became associated with Paul C. Pelz. The latter was a native of Silesia whose father was a noted historian but who found it advisable to come to the United States because of the revolutionary movements in Germany. The son studied at The College of The Holy Spirit and the College of Saint Elizabeth in Breslau before he rejoined his father in this country.

Smithmeyer and Pelz competed for the Library of Congress and received first place. The project languished and it is recorded that they were required to enter twelve different competitions and with forty-one competitors but in each competition they were victorious. Finally they received the commission to begin the work. Many European libraries were visited and every effort was made to have the building embody all the good features that had been developed. When the work on construction was started Smithmeyer was in charge. He objected to the quality of the cement that was being used and soon was dismissed from the work and replaced by a member of the United States Engineers. The architects sued for a payment of their commission based on a three per cent fee. They were awarded forty-eight thousand dollars. After thirteen years when the case was appealed to the Supreme Court, the architects were awarded a six-year salary of eight thousand dollars a year and payment of draughting and office expense. At Mr. Smithmeyer's death in 1908 no appropriation had been made for the payment of this award. The National Government in this case as in that of Major L'Enfant seems to have found a way to secure architectural services of the highest order without adequate payment.

Other works of the firm were the Healey Building at Georgetown University; the Carnegie Library at Allegheny, Pa. and many other large buildings. At the death of Mr. Smithmeyer a contemporary wrote: "He possessed a charming personality, never complaining at this affliction and adversity but with a heart full of sunshine. From him and him alone emanated the plan of the Library."

At his death March 14, 1908 the respect held for him was shown by the bearers selected for his funeral who were Senators William Steward of Nevada, Thomas Carter of Montana, J. H. Gallinger of New Hampshire, T. S. Martin of West Virginia and the architects Glenn Brown and Edward Donn. He was the oldest member of the A.I.A. and had been President of the Washington Chapter for three terms.

ADRIAN W. SMITH was born in Cincinnati Dec. 6, 1860. He was a son of Gen. Thomas Kilby Smith who had come from Massachusetts where his family had been settled since the middle of the sixteenth century. Adrian's health did not permit him to attend college but he was trained in the office of an architect in Baltimore. His brother was a distinguished lawyer, Walter George Smith, who was one of the outstanding Catholic laymen of the first half of the 20th century. During the architect's brief life he designed the Convent of The Visitation in Wilmington, Del.; the Convent of The Sacred Heart in Torresdale, Pa.; and Saint Elizabeth's Convent in Cornwells, Pa. He designed a number of crucifixes and worked upon the interior design of the chapel of the Industrial School at Eddington, Pa. He wrote a book of verse: *Thalassa and other Poems*. Died Dec. 18, 1892.

HAYDEN SMITH of Irish parentage was reared with a great hatred of anything Catholic. His father on his death bed enjoined on him the duty of avoiding anything Catholic even to the extent of not living in a town where there were any Catholics. The son was determined to carry out his father's wishes and during his early years went from city to city in England, Ireland, Canada the United States. Wherever he went he found a cross and Catholics.

PLATE LVI. The Library of Congress, Washington, D. C. Smithmeyer and Pelz, Architects.

Finally in western Pennsylvania where there was great antipathy to anything Catholic he found a book called *Defense of Catholic Principles*. This had been written by the priest who was born Prince Gallitzen of Russia and who had become a Catholic and came to America to work in the wilds of Western Pennsylvania. The architect's first impulse at seeing the book was to destroy it but he thought it would give him material to refute the beliefs of Catholicity. He read it, believed and soon after became a Catholic. The rest of his life he spent designing Catholic buildings such as the church at Loretto and Saint Mary's at Lancaster, Pa. At the time of his death he was working upon the improvement of Central Park in New York.

JOHN B. STACK was born in 1858 and was in practice in Baltimore, Md. where he designed the churches of Saint Ann; Saint Mary, Star of the Sea; Saint Charles; Saint Gregory and Saint Paul. Died August 18, 1932.

WILLIAM C. STANTON was a native of Philadelphia born in 1888. He was graduated in architecture from the University of Pennsylvania in 1907. He was employed by Philadelphia architects and was an engineer for the Zoning Commission. He made preliminary plans for the City Hall Annex in 1923. He served as Assistant Director for the Department of City Architecture in 1930 and 1931. From 1933 to 1935 he was the architect with the City Planning Commission. At his death he was a member of the firm of Folsom and Stanton. A member of the K. of C. and the A.I.A. Died Aug. 4, 1942.

JOHN C. STEPHENS was born in Iron Mountain, Mo. Sept. 16, 1870. He studied at Washington University and then entered the office of Isaac Taylor with whom he was associated the rest of his life. A member of the Saint Louis Artists' Guild, the Architectural Club, the K. of C. and the A.I.A. Died in 1951.

WILLIAM LA BARTHE STEELE was born in Springfield, Ill. on May 2, 1875. Of a mixed descent, his father being of Scotch, Irish and Pennsylvania Dutch ancestry and his mother who was a teacher of music being of Irish, French and English ancestry.

He was a graduate of the Springfield High School being class valedictorian and he received the degree of B. S. in architecture from the University of Illinois in 1896. He worked as a draftsman in Chicago in the office of Louis Sullivan and of S. S. Beman and in Pittsburgh with Thomas Rodd, Alden and Harlow and S. F. Heckert. Later he came to work in Sioux City, Ia. and after a year with W. W. Beach became his partner. This lasted but a short time and he practiced alone for twenty years. He then went to Omaha and became a member of the firm of Kimball, Steele and Sandham. This firm did much work in Iowa, Nebraska and the Dakotas. Among the buildings are Woodbury County Hospital; Saint Vincent's Church and the Church of The Sacred Heart in Sioux City, Ia. With Purcell and Emslie of Chicago the County Court House in Iowa City, Ia. With Thomas Kimball he worked upon the Cathedral of Saint Cecelia in Omaha.

In addition to his architectural work he engaged in many civic and professional activities: a four minute speaker in World War I; Reserve Officers' Association; one time President of the Iowa Chapter of the A.I.A.; member of the Board of Directors and a second Vice President; member of the State Board of Directors and a second Vice President; member of the State Board of Registration for Engi-

PLATE LVII. Church of The Sacred Heart, Pittsburgh, Pennsylvania. Carlton Strong, Architect. (Photograph by Johnston & Johnston.)

neers and Architects; member of the Library Board of Sioux City; District Officer for Nebraska and Kansas Historic Building Survey; K. of C.; contributor to Ecclesiastical Review; member of the Mayor's Housing Committee; Fellow of the A.I.A. Died in Neillsville, Wis. March 5, 1949.

GUSTAVE ERWIN STEINBACK was born in New York City in 1879 and was sent to Germany for his earlier education. Returning to this country he attended the Brooklyn Polytechnic Institute and was graduated in 1900 in architecture from Columbia University.

He was associated with other architects in New York and Brooklyn and designed some notable ecclesiastical work. Among these buildings are Saint Cecelia church and school in Stamford, Conn.; Saint Catherine of Siena church and rectory in Riverside, Conn.; the entire parish group of Saints Peter and Paul in Mount Vernon, N. Y.; a bishop's house in the Bahamas; the Cathedral of Saint Agnes in Rockville Centre, N. Y.; the church of The Blessed Sacrament in New York City; the church and school of All Saints in Brooklyn and the Quigley Seminary in Chicago. In the latter he was associated with Zachary Taylor Davis who acted as his representative in Chicago. At the time of his death he was designing an addition to the Roger Smith Hotel in Stamford, Conn.

He was a member of the A.I.A.; the Stamford Museum and Nature Centre; the American Museum of Natural History and the Metropolitan Museum of Art. A member of the 23rd Regiment of the New York National Guard. His death occurred due to being struck by a car September 24, 1959.

GEORGE H. STREETON was born in Brooklyn, N. Y. September 28, 1864. He studied at the Ferrari Modeling School, at Cooper Union and at Cornell University. Afterward for a decade he was employed by Schickel and Ditmars before engaging in his own practice. Among his buildings are Saint Ambrose and the Cathedral of Saint James in Brooklyn.

CARLTON STRONG was born in Lockport, N. Y. in 1862. He practiced in Pittsburgh from 1906 until his death. He had started his practice in Buffalo in 1888 and there made the first use of reinforced concrete in the Greystone Hotel. Then in the Markeen Hotel he used long span tile beams and concrete floor. He was the architect of many churches; the Bellefield Dwellings; the Rittenhouse Hotel in East Liberty; Mount Mercy Academy in Pittsburgh; Seton Hall College in Greensburg, Pa. and Saint Vincent's College in Latrobe, Pa. The Church of The Sacred Heart in East Liberty is an outstanding example of his work. Died June 26, 1931.

FRANCIS PAUL SULLIVAN was born in Washington, D. C. June 25, 1885, the son of Thomas and Catherine Connolly Sullivan. He was educated at Georgetown University where he received the degree of A.B. in 1904. Later he studied at George Washington University until 1909. He was a member of the firm of Wyeth and Sullivan. His military service was as a Captain in the Ordnance Reserve Corps; Major in the Reserve Corps. From 1923 until 1926 he was Comptroller of the P. O. Department; Consultant on the U. S. Capitol, House and Senate Office Buildings; east wing of the Senate Office Building; Afghanistan Embassy. Member of the Board of Trade; Phi Sigma Kappa; Fellow of the A.I.A.; Cosmos Club of Washington; Delegate to Congress of Architects in Paris in 1937; Chairman of the A.I.A. Committee on the National Capitol. Author of articles on architecture and city planning; a novel; member of the Society of Architectural Historians. Died Feb. 5, 1958.

128

PLATE LVIII. Providence College, Providence, Rhode Island. Matthew Sullivan, Architect. (Photograph courtesy of Providence College News Bureau.)

MATTHEW SULLIVAN was born in Boston in 1868 and was educated there. He was trained in the office of Edmund Wheelwright who was architect of the public schools. Later he became his assistant and successor in 1895. In 1901 he became a member of the firm of Maginnis, Walsh and Sullivan. This lasted until his withdrawal in 1930. In this period many important buildings were designed such as the Church of The Sacred Heart in Taunton, Mass.; Saint Mark's in Dorchester; Saint Rose of Lima in Chelsea; the Boston Teachers' College and the Girls' Latin School; Saint John's Preparatory School in Danvers. After leaving the firm his work included the College of The Sacred Heart in Providence and Providence College. Died Aug. 12, 1948.

JAMES SWEENEY was born in New York in 1870 and was trained in offices there. In New London, Conn. where he established an office he was architect of the Municipal Building; the Union Bank Building; Saint Mary's Convent and parish school. Died July 3, 1919.

A. BERNARD THUMEL was born in Maryland and was educated at the Tome Institute and studied at the University of Pennsylvania. He worked in offices in Pittsburgh and during World War I served as a major in the Army. Died in 1955.

JOHN KINNEY TINGLEY was born in 1911 in Norwich, Conn. the son of Doctor Witter K. and Frances Ryan Tingley. He was graduated from the Norwich Free Academy in 1930 and from the Department of Architecture at Notre Dame with honors in 1935. He was an excellent water colorist and was rapidly advancing in his profession at the time of his death, Nov. 10, 1939.

ALBERT TOLEDANO was born in New Orleans in 1859 and attended school there. He worked for James Freret and later with Thomas Sully. He became well known for his work and was looked upon as one of the best informed architects in the city and the South.

   Later he was associated with Victor Wogan. Among the buildings from their office were the Hutchinson Memorial Building and the Water Board Building. He was a member of the Louisiana Club and the Boston Club. Died July 18, 1923.

COLONEL TOUSSAR was with L'Enfant and designed Fort William in the Delaware River.

PATRICK A. TRACY was in practice in Boston during the early years of the 20th century.

JESUS TREVINO was working at the Mission of San Ygacio, Tex. during its early years.

TRISCINI an Italian-Swiss architect was working in Natchitoches, La. during the 1830's where there are many buildings attributed to him.

PETER TROLIO of Jackson, Miss. received his early education there and was graduated from the University of Notre Dame in architecture and returned to Jackson where he was in practice until his death Sept. 29, 1951.

130 FRANK JOSEPH UNTERSEE was born in 1858 and he was educated in his native town of Glarus,

PLATE LIX. Cathedral of Saint Helena, Helena, Montana. Albert von Herbulis, Architect. (Photograph by Jorud Photo.)

131

Switzerland. He was sent to Germany for technical training at Stuttgart University. Afterward he was employed by the City Architect of Berne before coming to the United States in 1882.

He worked mostly in the vicinity of Boston where he designed in Brookline a number of public buildings. He was soon employed in ecclesiastical work doing a great number of churches and schools. He was the architect of Saint Patrick's Church in Jaffrey, N. H.; Saint Lawrence Church in Brookline; Saint Anthony's in Allston, Mass.; Saint Peter and Paul in Jamestown, N. Y.; buildings for the Redemptorist Fathers at Esopus, N. Y. and for the Mission Church in Roxbury, Mass. He was a member of the Boston Society of Architects and the A.I.A. Died Sept. 9, 1927.

WYBEE van der MEER was born in Friesland, The Netherlands, and came to Aurora, Ill. In this part of the state he designed a number of buildings as Marmion and Madonna High Schools in Saint Charles, Ill.; Saint Vincent Orphanage in Freeport; Saint Joseph Hospital in Aurora; The Sacred Heart Seminary at Geneva, Ill.; and Muldoon and Saint Thomas High Schools. A member of the Illinois Society of Architects. Died 1948.

JAMES R. VEEDER was born in 1883 in Syracuse, N. Y. He was a graduate of Massachusetts Institute of Technology in 1907. Later he was associated with the firm of Randall and Veeder in 1916 and in 1949 with Veeder and Curtin and retired in 1957.

He and his associates were architects for many public buildings including Grant Junior High School; Eastwood Homes; Syracuse Housing Authority and Loretto Rest.

He was a trustee of the Cathedral of The Immaculate Conception in Syracuse; a member of the Rotary Club; Saint Mary's Men's Club; former president and secretary of the Syracuse Society of Architects; former secretary and member emeritus of the Central New York Chapter of the A.I.A.; chairman of the Onondaga Public Works Commission. Died in August 1959.

FATHER PETER VERHEYDEN S. J. who was pastor of the College Church in Saint Louis in 1839 until 1842 is given as the architect of the church which was built at that time. Charles Dickens who saw the building in this period stated in his "American Notes" that "the architect of this building is one of the Reverend Fathers of the School and the works proceed under his sole direction." It was evidently based upon Greek and Roman motives judging from contemporary accounts.

CHRISTIAN G. VIERHEILIG was born in Bavaria on Dec. 20, 1867. He came to the United States at the age of thirteen and went directly to Grand Rapids, Mich. Here he received his training and began his practice. His work was largely ecclesiastical. He was the architect for the first buildings at Saint Mary's Hospital and for many churches in Michigan including Saint Isadore in Grand Rapids, Saint Mary's in New Salem, Saint Francis in Holland and many church interiors. Died Feb. 19, 1931.

ALBERT von HERBULIS was born in Budapest April 23, 1860. He was graduated from the Military Academy and from the Polytechnicum at Vienna with the degree of Bachelor of Science in Architecture. After coming to this country he worked in Pittson, Pa. as a mining engineer. After five years in mining he began his work as an architect in Scranton and then went to Washington, D. C. where he remained the rest of his life. He did much work throughout the country. Included in this are such buildings

PLATE LX. Cathedral of the Blessed Sacrament, Detroit, Michigan. Henry Walsh, Architect. (Photograph by The Detroit News.)

as the Cathedral in Helena, Montana; the Art and Science Building at the University of Ottawa, Can.; the Pensacola Hospital in Florida; Community House at Notre Dame; Holy Cross College; the Marist College and the Dominican House of Studies at the Catholic University; Saint Charles College and Saint Charles School in Helena; Ryan Hall and dormitories at Georgetown University; Holy Angels Academy and school in Buffalo; the Convent of Perpetual Adoration in Birmingham, Ala.; the House of Studies in Coleman, Ala. Some of his churches include Saint James, Falls Church, Va.; The Sacred Heart in Old Point Comfort, Va.; a church at Deer Lodge, Mont. In New York he remodelled Saint Peter's on Barclay Street. Died April 14, 1928.

JOSSE A. VRYDAGH was born in Louvain, Belgium May 16, 1833. He was the son of Peter and Mary Vrydagh. His father was a soldier with Napoleon and fought at the battle of Liepaic. After his military service he was a wholesale grocer and manufacturer of spices. He was greatly desirous that his son should become a priest so much so that he took away the boy's drawing instruments and sent him to a seminary. Before the boy was fourteen he left the seminary and worked for a civil engineer in Paris and then returning to Louvain he spent seven years studying at the School of Fine Arts in the city.

He left Europe in 1854 and went to Dallas, Texas where he lived for a period engaged upon architecture and contracting. The Saint Nicholas Hotel which was the outstanding hotel of the city was his work while in Dallas. In 1860 he returned to Europe and visited many of the cities of France, Belgium and Holland and in 1862 went to the World's Fair in London. It was in this period that he married in Louvain and returned to America and until 1866 was living in Cincinnati. He then moved to Terre Haute, Indiana where he spent the remainder of his life.

He did much work in southern Indiana and among the buildings the following: Saint Joseph's and Saint Patrick's churches in Terre Haute; the Catholic Orphan Home; The Terre Haute House; Wiley High School; buildings at Depauw University in Greencastle; court houses in Bedford, Sullivan and Mount Vernon, Indiana and many public and private buildings at Evansville.

In 1870 he became a Fellow of the A.I.A. In 1874 he submitted designs for buildings at the Centennial Exposition in Philadelphia and among fifty competitors he received one of the ten prizes offered. In 1877 he received an award of a thousand dollars from the Federal Government for a design for rebuilding the Patent Office. For a period he was in the Supervising Architect's office in Washington. He submitted designs for the Sailors' and Soldiers' Monument in Indianapolis and for the State Capitol. His three sons entered his office and practiced with him and now the office represents almost a century of tradition. Died 1898.

JAMES WAHRENBERGER was born in Austin, Texas of German parents. He studied at technical schools in Europe and practiced for a few years in Austin before moving to San Antonio.

In the latter city he did much work such as the first building of Our Lady of the Lake College, buildings at Saint Louis College which is now Saint Mary's University, the Alamo Bank Building, the Reuter Building, Turner Hall. He was architect for many of the school buildings of the city and the first City Building Inspector. Died 1928.

DAVID A. CLARKE WAGGAMAN was born Nov. 16, 1877. He studied at Georgetown and later in Europe. His work was largely residential, some of it being restorations of historic houses. He also worked

PLATE LXI. Maryknoll, New York. Catholic Foreign Mission Society of America. Maginnis and Walsh, Architects.

upon housing for the Navy Department. A member of the Metropolitan Club and Chevy Chase and Montgomery Country Clubs. Died in Oct. 1919.

HENRY AUGUSTINE WALSH was born in 1868. He studied in Cleveland and later in Europe. An excellent pianist he was recognized as a man of refinement and good taste which was shown in his architectural work. He worked for several important firms in Cleveland before undertaking his own work. He was architect for a number of churches and schools. Among these are the Church of Our Lady of Good Counsel; Saint Mary's in Mentor, Ohio; Saint Agnes in Elyria, Ohio; a monastery in Detroit and the Cathedral of The Blessed Sacrament in the same city. A member of the A.I.A. Died Jan. 5, 1940.

JAMES R. WALSH came to Florida about the beginning of the 20th century and worked for many years in Jacksonville where he was the architect for many of the important buildings of the city in that period. A member of the Holy Name Society and social organizations. Died November 12, 1924.

ROBERT W. WALSH was a son of Thomas Walsh and an associate of Frederick Widman in the design of many industrial buildings in Saint Louis and Chicago. An early member of the Western Association of Architects and a Fellow of the A.I.A. Died in 1929.

THOMAS WALSH was born in Kilkenny, Ireland Feb. 15, 1826 a son of William Walsh who was an architect in that city. He studied in Dublin with William Dean Butler and at an early age came to the United States. From 1850 he was active professionally for forty years in Saint Louis. He was the architect for the Fallon Polytechnic School where architectural courses where offered, the first in the city; the Lindell Hotel; the Four Courts; Saint John's Church and the Federal Building. Died in March, 1890.

THOMAS F. WALSH was born in Chicago, Aug. 5, 1866 a son of John and Alice Bailey Walsh. He was educated at Holy Trinity parish school; he entered the office of Trest and Foltz until he went to work for Edbrooke and Burnham. After six years in Chicago offices he went to Denver to work for R. S. Roeschlaub. He again came to Chicago where he was head designer for Holabird and Roche on such buildings as the Monadnock Building; the Old Colony and the Marquette Buildings. He returned to Denver in April 1894 where he was associated with Aaron M. Gove for the remainder of his life. Died early in the 20th century.

TIMOTHY FRANCIS WALSH was born in Cambridge, Mass. in 1868. He was graduated from the Boston English School in 1886. He worked for a number of years in Boston offices and spent a year in Paris and another year in travel. In 1896 he joined Charles D. Maginnis and Matthew Sullivan and the firm took a high place in architecture. The competition for the New buildings at Boston College gave them first prize. Then followed a number of important buildings as Trinity College Chapel in Washington, D. C.; the Maryknoll Mother House in Ossining, N. Y. the founder of the Maryknoll Fathers being Bishop Walsh, the brother of the architect; the Carmelite Convent in Santa Clara, Calif.; Saint Catherine of Siena Church in Somerville, Mass.; Maryknoll Seminary in Los Gatos, Calif.; Saint Gregory's Seminary in Cincinnati. He was President of the Boston Board of Appeals and a Fellow of the A.I.A. Died July 7, 1934.

T. WALSH was architect of the Church of The Most Holy Redeemer on 3rd Street between Aves. A and B, N. Y. City.

THOMAS J. WELSH was born in Australia in 1845. He was brought to California where he was educated in the public schools and at Saint Ignatius·College. He was a member of the K. of C. and the A.I.A. and prominent in public service.

ANTHONY WEWER was born at Harsewinkel in Westphalia, Germany, April 14, 1836. On July 14th, 1860 he became a member of the Franciscan Order and received the name of Brother Adrian. In 1862 he came to the United States and to the Midwest where he devoted much of the remaining fifty years of his life to the designing of churches and convents. He removed to California where he died March 15, 1914.

ALPHEUS WHITE of Cincinnati was the architect of The Athenaeum in 1830 which was a day and boarding school later developing to college grade. It was razed in 1890.

In 1833 Bishop Fenwick who had brought Mr. White into The Church died during a cholera epidemic in Wooster, Ohio and after a brief period the architect supervised the removal of the Bishop's body to his Cathedral in Cincinnati.

FATHER GILBERT WINKELMANN, O. S. B. was born May 21, 1889 in Saint Paul, Minn. He attended the Assumption school whose parish church was designed by the distinguished Austrian architect, Riedell, and after leaving the parish school he entered Saint John's Preparatory School and then attended Saint John's University where he received a degree of A. B. in music. This always remained an interest to him as he was an accomplished pianist and organist and for a short while he taught music. In 1909 he entered Saint John's Abbey and was professed a monk July 16, 1910. In 1916 he was ordained a priest. He attended summer courses at the Art Institute in Chicago, Armour Institute and the University of Chicago. From the latter he received a Master of Science degree in mathematics in 1925. His interest in mathematics is shown by his development of a mechanical device for solving complicated problems in trigonometry with rapidity and ease. He also developed his "beam theory" in compound definite integrals. His ability as a teacher is shown by the Army Air Force after the cadets whom he had instructed rated highest in the recognition given by a special citation from the country on the air forces' comprehensive tests.

However, his greatest interest had always been in architecture and he began a school of architecture at Saint John's and designed a number of churches including those in Avon, Swanville and Foxhome in Minnesota and Rugby and Fort Totten in North Dakota. In World War II he developed a camouflage for radar towers which proved most effective. He was a member of the A.I.A.; the Minnesota Association of Architects and the Mathematical Association of America. His last work was as a pastor of the church in Saint Martin where because of his health he had been assigned shortly before his death in 1946.

VICTOR WOGAN was born in New Orleans in 1870 the son of Charles and Adeline Wogan. He was graduated with the degree of A. B. in 1887 at the College of The Immaculate Conception—now Loyola

University—and later studied at Louisiana State University. He began the practice of architecture with Albert Toledano in 1893. After the death of the latter he was associated with Bernard until his own death. Among his earlier buildings were the Elks' Home; the Bienville Apartments; the Grunewald Hotel; buildings at Xavier University; Louisiana State University and the Court House and High School at Houma, La.

He was President of the Lousiana Chapter of the A. I. A. His death occurred June 4, 1953 and the funeral was at Our Lady of Lourdes Church in New Orleans.

JOHN WALTER WOOD was born in 1900. Educated at Harvard where he received a B. S. degree in 1922 and a Master in Architecture degree in 1927. He studied at Oxford in 1923 and at the Ecole des Beaux Arts in Paris in 1928.

He practiced architecture and especially air port design from 1931. He was architect for the Air Force School in Denver; consultant on air ports to the Assistant Secretary of Commerce and from 1943 until 1945 airport analyst for the Port of New York Authority. He was chief of the layout and safety unit, airport development and engineering branch at headquarters of the Army Air Force in 1945.
He held airport patents in the United States, Canada, Britain and France. Author of *Airports—Some Elements of Design and Future Development* and *Airports and Air Traffic*. A Fellow of the American Geographical Society, an associate of the Institute of Aeronautical Sciences and a member of the A.I.A.; the Liturgical Arts Society and the New York State Association of Architects. Associate Professor of Architecture at the University of Illinois from 1948. Died in 1958.

PADRE JOSE MARIA DE ZALVIDEA was at San Gabriel from 1802 until 1826 and was considered skillful administrator and probably had much to do with the building of the Mission. He was born at Bilbao, Vizcaya on March 2, 1780 and died at San Gabriel in 1846.

WLADYSLAUS H. ZAWADZKI was born in 1872 and practiced in Buffalo for many years. He was the architect of many churches and schools including the Polish Home and the Union Home. Died Jan. 18, 1926.

DON FRANCISCO ZAPARY is described in a note inserted in the Cathedral records by Father Antonio in Dec. 1825 as an Italian painter and architect who worked upon the Cathedral of New Orleans.

Information on the following individuals was received too late to be included in the alphabetical listing.

FRANK BARTOLOMEI was born in Italy and came to Chicago many years before the Chicago Fire of 1871. He did much work upon the interiors of the Church of the Assumption; Church of Notre Dame; Saint Jarlath's Church, all in Chicago. His work embraced many theatres and ecclesiastical structures in this country and Mexico. He worked upon the Egyptian Village built for the World's Fair of 1893. He had other interests such as the patenting of a material for use in interior decoration and he invented a vending machine, perhaps the first such machine and which was used in the City Hall. While in Europe regarding his patents in England, France, and Germany, he died March 26, 1898 and was buried in Lucca, Italy.

FRANCIS BARTOLOMEI, his nephew who later changed his name to Barton, was trained by his uncle and became well known in Chicago for his work. Among his buildings is the Edgewater Beach Hotel. He also was an inventor and developed the steel web system for tall buildings. He designed and advocated the building of tall buildings over open spaces such as over railroad tracks but this too advanced an idea for the period. He died in 1930.

FREDERICK P. DINKELBERG was born in 1861 at Lancaster, Pa. and studied in Philadelphia later coming to Chicago where he was employed in the office of D.H. Burnham. While there he worked upon many of the important buildings of that office. Died February 18, 1935.

THOMAS F. IMBS was born in Saint Louis, Mo. August 17, 1885. He studied at Saint Louis University and at Washington University before entering the University of Pennsylvania where he received in 1910 the degrees of B.S. in Arch. and B.S. in Arch. Eng. He was associated with John Comes on the design of the Catholic seminary in Saint Louis and later practiced alone.
   Author of *Architects Contracts; Principles of Modern Bank Architecture* and *Theory of Church Arrchitecture*. Member of the Wisconsin and Illinois Society of Architects; Society of Engineers and K. of C. Died 1959.

J. HENRY MEYER was born in Wapakoneta, Ohio May 9, 1889 and was educated in the schools of the town and later attended Ohio State University at Columbus. He engaged in a general architectural and engineering practice. He served as County Surveyor and City Engineer and engaged in many business and community projects. He was the author of *Atlas of Auglaize County, 1910* and *Atlas and History of Auglaize County 1917*. Member of K. of C.; Kappa Sigma and other social organizations. Died 1940.

JOHN C. RIEDELL was born in Paris, Illinois Sept. 27, 1909. Attended the local schools and Peddie School in New Jersey and then entered the architectural department of the University of Notre Dame. He was employed in Indiana offices before beginning his own practice. Died in Paris, March 14, 1950.
RORBET J. REILEY was born in New York City Sept. 26, 1878. He studied at St. Francis Xavier College and entered Columbia University where he received his architectural degree in 1900.

LOUIS HENRI SULLIVAN was born in Boston, Sept. 13, 1852. His father was Patrick Sullivan from Dublin, Ireland where he had been a dancing teacher and also in Paris. When he came to Boston he followed the same work until his removal to Chicago. The mother was of German stock from Alsace-Lorraine and she was an artist of ability. This union did not give a marked religious trend to the son but it did give a child of marked artistic ability.

He studied in the Boston schools and later was a student at the Massachusetts Institute of Technology. For about a year he was in Philadelphia where he came under the influence of Furness who was known as a robust designer. Sullivan joined his parents in Chicago and then went to France to study at the Ecole des Beaux Arts. Atelier life seemed to be congenial for he remained two years before returning to Chicago.

He then became associated with Dankmar Adler and the firm gradually became known for an extensive practice during the last two decades of the 19th century and into the 20th century. At this time Sullivan was recognized as an outstanding designer and was probably responsible for such buildings as the Transportation Building at the World's Fair of 1893. This was a brilliant design and among some of the less spectacular buildings were the Auditorium Hotel and the Auditorium. The hotel is now occupied by Roosevelt University and the Auditorium seems destined to be saved from the tools of the wrecker. The Garrick Theatre now razed; the Carson Pirie-Scott Department Store shows the beauty of the system of ornamentation that characterized his work.

In Saint Louis were a number of buildings and among them the Wainright Building that illustrates his theory that " form should follow function " as does the Guaranty or Prudential Building in Buffalo.

The later years of his life were largely spent alone but during this period he designed some interesting bank buildings; especially one in Owatonna, Minn.

He was the author of: *An Autobiography of an Idea* and *A System of Architectural Ornament*. Died in Chicago, April 11, 1924.